the **vegetarian** student cookbook

the vegetarian student cookbook

GREAT GRUB FOR THE HUNGRY AND THE BROKE

RYLAND PETERS & SMALL
LONDON • NEW YORK

Senior Designer Iona Hoyle

Senior Editor Céline Hughes

Picture Research Emily Westlake

Production Controller Maria Petalidou

Art Director Leslie Harrington

Publishing Director Alison Starling

Indexer Penelope Kent

First published in the US in 2010
This revised edition published in 2017
by Ryland Peters & Small
341 E 116th St
New York, NY 10029
www.rylandpeters.com

10 9 8 7 6 5 4 3

Text © Nadia Arumugam, Fiona Beckett, Vatcharin
Bhumichitr, Celia Brooks Brown, Tamsin Burnett-Hall, Maxine
Clark, Linda Collister, Ross Dobson, Ursula Ferrigno, Liz
Franklin, Clare Ferguson, Manisha Gambhir Harkins, Tonia
George, Brian Glover, Nicola Graimes, Kate Habershon,
Rachael Anne Hill, Caroline Marson, Jane Noraika, Louise
Pickford, Rena Salaman, Jennie Shapter, Fiona Smith, Sonia
Stevenson, Sunil Vijayakar, Fran Warde, Laura Washburn,
Lindy Wildsmith, and Ryland Peters & Small 2010

Design and photographs © Ryland Peters & Small 2010, 2017

ISBN: 978-1-84975-887-1

Printed and bound in China

A CIP record for this book is available from
the Library of Congress.

Notes:
- All spoon measurements are level, unless otherwise specified.

- Ovens should be preheated to the specified temperature. Recipes in this book were tested using a regular oven. If using a convection oven, follow the manufacturer's instructions for adjusting temperatures.

- All eggs are medium, unless otherwise specified. Recipes containing raw or partially cooked egg should not be served to the very young, very old, anyone with a compromised immune system, or pregnant women.

contents

Now that you're a fully fledged student and embracing independence, you're going to want to know how to cook up a storm in the kitchen. *The Vegetarian Student Cookbook* is here to allay any fears you might have about cooking veggie food for yourself. Some of the recipes are super-quick, while others need time to work their magic. Either way, they are stress-free and designed to satisfy, whether you're coming home late with a mammoth hunger after a night out, or you're having friends over for a lazy Sunday lunch. You'll soon realize that veggie food isn't dull or time-consuming and that there are lots of easy and tasty dishes you can whip up. Check out the tips in the first few pages before you get started—they will make life a lot easier and ensure that your culinary efforts are always successful, undaunting, and above all, fun.

introduction

kitchen know-how

The recipes in this book need the minimum of kitchen equipment. Some recipes, like the desserts, will require extras, e.g. a handheld electric whisk (which can be bought very cheaply), a baking pan for brownies, etc. but you can go a long way with these essentials:

2 or 3 sharp knives, including a serrated knife

wooden spoon

fish/egg slice

potato masher

garlic crusher

pepper mill

can opener

vegetable peeler

cheese grater

2 cutting boards (1 for meat-eating friends to use and 1 for veg)

large mixing bowl

strainer

colander

1 large and 1 medium saucepan

skillet with a lid

baking sheet

roasting pan

ovenproof dish (Pyrex or ceramic)

measuring cups

weighing scales

a selection of airtight containers

kettle

toaster

aluminum foil

plastic wrap

baking parchment

paper towels

cleaning stuff, including washing up liquid, sponges, and surface cleaner

kitchen towels

oven gloves

Every recipe has at least one of these symbols:

 serves 4 This tells you roughly how many people the recipe should serve.

 Q This is an extra-quick recipe, and shouldn't take you longer than 20 minutes once you've prepared the ingredients.

vegetarian tips

• Cheeses started with animal rennet are not suitable for strict vegetarians, so read food labeling carefully and check that the cheese you buy is made with a non-animal starter. Traditional Parmesan is not suitable, so where it is specified in a recipe, substitute any vegetarian hard cheese that can be grated, Parma (a vegan product), or nutritional yeast flakes. Similarly, Gorgonzola is not vegetarian, so you should look for a Gorgonzola-style soft blue cheese.

• Some brands of Worcestershire sauce contain anchovies, so check that the one you buy is labeled as suitable for vegetarians.

• If you are sharing a kitchen with meat-eaters, always keep meat and vegetable cutting boards separate.

handy ingredients

sea salt

black peppercorns

olive oil

vegetable or
safflower oil

balsamic vinegar

red or white wine
vinegar

dark or light soy sauce

tomato ketchup (as if
you needed reminding!)

mustard

mayonnaise

long grain rice

risotto rice

dried pasta,
including spaghetti

couscous

vegetable stock cubes
or bouillon powder

canned chopped
tomatoes

a selection of canned
beans, such as
cannellini, kidney

all-purpose flour

sugar

tomato paste

a selection of dried
herbs, such as oregano

a selection of dried
spices, such as curry
powder, ground cumin,
paprika, chili powder,
or hot red pepper flakes

dried porcini
mushrooms

honey

butter or margarine

milk

onions

garlic

food safety

• The first rule of cooking is to always keep your kitchen clean! Keep it tidy and disinfect worktops after use with a mild detergent or an antibacterial cleaner. Keep pets off surfaces and, as far as possible, keep them out of the kitchen.

• Store food safely to avoid cross-contamination. Keep food in clean, dry, airtight containers, always store raw and cooked foods separately, and wash utensils (and your hands) between preparing raw and cooked foods.

• Wash your hands well with hot, soapy water before and after handling food.

• Never put hot food into a fridge, as this will increase the internal temperature to an unsafe level. Cool leftover food quickly to room temperature, ideally by transferring it to a cold dish, then refrigerate. Cool large dishes such as stews by putting the dish in a sink of cold water. Stir occasionally (change the water often to keep the temperature low), then refrigerate once cool. During cooling, cover the food loosely with plastic wrap to protect it from contamination.

• Don't use perishable food beyond the expiration date as it could be a health risk. If you have any doubts about the food, discard it.

• Reheated food must be piping hot throughout before consumption. Never reheat any type of food more than once.

• If you are going to freeze food, freeze food that is in prime condition, on the day of purchase, or as soon as a dish is made and cooled. Freeze it quickly and in small quantities, if possible. Label and date food and keep a good rotation of stock in the freezer.

• Always leave a gap in the container when freezing liquids, so that there is enough room for the liquid to expand as it freezes.

• Always let food cool before freezing it. Warm or hot food will increase the internal temperature of the freezer and may cause other foods to begin to defrost and spoil.

• Use proper oven gloves to remove hot dishes from the oven—don't just use a kitchen towel because you risk burning yourself. Kitchen towels are also a breeding ground for germs so only use them for drying, and wash them often.

• Hard cheeses such as cheddar, Gruyère, and Parmesan will keep for up to 3 weeks if stored correctly. Once opened, fresh, soft cheeses such as cream cheese should be consumed within 3 days.

• Wash hands before and after handling eggs, and discard any cracked and/or dirty eggs.

- If your kitchen is prone to over-heating, it is best to store eggs in their box in the fridge. Keep them pointed-end downward and away from strong-smelling foods, as they can absorb odors. Always use by expiration date.
- Leftover canned foods should be transferred to an airtight container, kept in the fridge, and eaten within 2 days. Once cans are opened, the contents should be treated as fresh food. This doesn't apply to food sold in tubs with resealable lids, such as cocoa powder.
- Cooked rice is a potential source of food poisoning. Cool leftovers quickly (ideally within an hour), then store in an airtight container in the fridge and use within 24 hours. Always reheat cooked cold rice until piping hot.
- The natural oils in chiles may cause irritation to your skin and eyes. When preparing them, wear disposable gloves or pull a small polythene bag over each hand, secured with an elastic band around the wrist, to create a glove.

ingredients tips

- Chop leftover fresh herbs, spoon them into an ice-cube tray, top with a little water, and freeze. Once solid, put the cubes in a freezer bag. Seal, label, and return to the freezer. Add the frozen herb cubes to soups, casseroles, and sauces.

- When substituting dried herbs for fresh, use roughly half the quantity the recipe calls for, as dried herbs have a more concentrated flavor.
- The color of a fresh chile is no indication of how hot it will be. Generally speaking, the smaller and thinner the chile, the hotter it will be.
- To reduce the heat of a fresh chile, cut it in half lengthwise, then scrape out and discard the seeds and membranes (or core). See also "food safety" above for advice on handling chiles.
- Most vegetables keep best in the fridge, but a cool, dark place is also good if you lack fridge space. Potatoes should always be stored in the dark, otherwise they go green or sprout, making them inedible.
- To skin tomatoes, score a cross in the base of each one using a sharp knife. Put them in a heatproof bowl, cover with boiling water, leave for about 30 seconds, then transfer them to a bowl of cold water. When cool enough to handle, drain and peel off the skins with a knife.
- To clean leeks, trim them, then slit them lengthwise about a third of the way through. Open the leaves a little and wash away any dirt from between the layers under cold running water.
- Store coffee (beans and ground) in the fridge or freezer, or it will go stale very quickly.

- Store flour in its original sealed packaging or in an airtight container in a cool, dry, airy place. Ideally, buy and store small quantities at a time, to help avoid infestation of psocids (very small, barely visible, gray-brown insects), which may appear even in the cleanest of homes. If you do find these small insects in your flour, dispose of it immediately and wash and dry the container thoroughly. Never mix new flour with old.
- If you run out of self-rising flour, sift 1 teaspoon baking powder with every cup of all-purpose flour. This will not be quite as effective but it is a good emergency substitute.
- Store oils, well sealed, in a cool, dark, dry place, away from direct sunlight. They can be kept in the fridge (though this is not necessary), but oils such as olive oil tend to solidify and go cloudy in the fridge. If this happens, bring the oil back to room temperature before use.
- Small pasta tubes and twists such as penne and fusilli are good for chunky vegetable sauces and some cream-based sauces. Smooth, creamy, butter- or olive oil-based sauces are ideal for long strands such as spaghetti (so the sauce can cling to the pasta).
- Dried pasta has a long shelf life and should be stored in its unopened package or in an airtight container in a cool, dry place.

Leftover cooked pasta should be kept in a sealed container in the fridge and used within 2 days. Ordinary cooked pasta does not freeze well on its own, but it freezes successfully in dishes such as lasagne and cannelloni. Allow 3–4 oz. dried pasta per person.

• Pasta must be cooked in a large volume of salted, boiling water. Keep the water at a rolling boil throughout cooking. Once you have added the pasta to the boiling water, give it a stir, then cover the pan to help the water return to the boil as quickly as possible. Remove the lid once the water has started boiling again (to prevent the water boiling over), and stir occasionally. Check the instructions on the package for cooking times. When it is ready, cooked pasta should be al dente—tender but still with a slight resistance.

• As an accompaniment, allow 2–3 oz. uncooked rice per person or for an entrée like risotto, up to 4 oz.

• Rice may be rinsed before cooking to remove tiny pieces of grit or excess starch. Most packaged rice is checked and clean, however, so rinsing it is unnecessary and will wash away nutrients. Risotto rice is not washed before use, but basmati rice usually is—rinse it under cold water until the water runs clear.

taste tips

• Try mixing a pinch or two of ground spices such as curry powder, chili powder, or turmeric with bread crumbs or flour, and use to coat foods before frying. Add ground spices such as cinnamon, apple pie spice, or ginger to fruit cobbler toppings. A pinch or two of grated nutmeg will perk up mashed potatoes, cheese sauce, cooked spinach, scrambled eggs, and rice puddings.

• Stir wholegrain mustard into mashed potatoes or mayonnaise before serving to add extra flavor. Mustard also enhances salad dressings and sauces. A pinch of mustard powder added to cheese dishes will enhance the flavor.

- If you add too much salt to a soup or casserole, add one or two peeled and cubed potatoes to soak up the salt, cooking until tender. Discard the potatoes before serving.
- An excellent way of thickening soups is to stir in a little oatmeal. It adds flavor and richness too. A small amount of instant mashed potato stirred in at the last minute is also a good way of thickening soup.
- Add a little pearl barley to soups and stews—it will add flavor and texture and have a thickening effect.
- A teaspoon or two of pesto sauce stirred into each portion of a hot vegetable soup just before serving will liven it up.
- For a tasty and creamy salad dressing, mash some blue cheese and stir it into mayonnaise, or a mixture of mayonnaise and plain Greek yogurt.
- Add some health and a satisfying crunch to salads by tossing in a handful or two of lightly toasted seeds or chopped nuts just before serving. Good ideas include sunflower, sesame, or pumpkin seeds and hazelnuts, walnuts, pecans, or pistachios. Toasted seeds can also be sprinkled over cooked vegetables.
- If you over-cook an omelet, let it cool and use it as a sandwich filling. Chop the omelet and combine it with mayonnaise and snipped chives, if you like.

- Bulk out a pasta or rice salad by adding a can of drained and rinsed beans such as chickpeas, red kidney beans, or black-eye beans.
- For an extra-tasty cobbler topping, replace 1 oz. of the flour with the same weight of chopped nuts, rolled oats, or oatmeal, or replace white sugar with coarse brown sugar.

kitchen wisdom

- To remove odors from a container that you want to use again, fill the container with hot water, then stir in 1 tablespoon baking powder. Let it stand overnight, then wash, rinse well, and dry before use.
- If you transfer foods from packages to storage containers, sellotape the food label onto the container so you can easily identify its contents and you have a record of the manufacturer's cooking instructions, if necessary. Make a note of the expiration date on the container, too.
- For convenient single servings, freeze portions of homemade soup in large, thick paper cups or small individual containers. Remove them from the freezer as required, defrost, and reheat the soup thoroughly before serving.
- To make salad dressings or vinaigrettes, put all the ingredients in a clean screw-top jar, seal, and shake well. Alternatively, put the ingredients straight into the salad bowl and whisk together well, before adding the salad.
- Spirits with an alcohol content of 35% or over can be kept in the freezer—this is ideal for those which should be served ice-cold.

microwave safety

- The more food you are cooking, and the colder it is, the longer it will take to cook in a microwave.
- Metal containers, china with a metal trim, foil, or crystal glass (which contains lead) should not be used in a microwave. Metal reflects microwaves and may damage the oven components. Microwave-safe plastic containers, ovenproof glass, and ceramic dishes are all suitable, as is most household glazed china. Paper plates and paper towels can be used to reheat food for short periods. Roasting bags (pierced) may be used in a microwave.
- Many foods need to be covered during microwaving. Use microwave-safe plastic wrap, a plate, or a lid. Pierce plastic wrap, or leave a gap at one side if using a plate or lid, to allow excess steam to escape.
- Use a microwave with a built-in turntable if possible, and make sure that you stir the food several times during cooking to ensure even cooking throughout. The food on the outer edges usually cooks first.

- Never operate a microwave when it is empty, as the microwaves will bounce back to and damage the oven components.
- Be careful when stirring heated liquids in a container in the microwave, as they can bubble up without warning.
- After food has been removed from the microwave, it will continue to cook due to the residual heat within the food, so adhere to standing times when they are given in recipes.
- Take care when removing the cover from a microwave container as the steam inside will be very hot.

light bites and sides

spicy lentil dip

spicy *lentil* dip

Lentils contain loads of great things—protein, fiber, zinc, and more—and they are also very filling, so they make an ideal base for a snack or meal. Serve with crudités or pita bread.

1¼ cups red lentils

2 tablespoons butter

1 small onion, finely chopped

1–2 tablespoons curry powder

salt and black pepper

freshly chopped cilantro, to serve (optional)

Put the lentils and 1¾ cups water in a saucepan. Bring to a boil, reduce the heat, and simmer for 20–30 minutes, until the water is absorbed. Remove from the heat and mash with a fork.

Melt the butter in a small saucepan, add the onion, and cook gently for about 5 minutes, until soft but not colored. Add the curry powder and cook for a further 1–2 minutes. Add the mashed lentils to the pan, stir, and cook for 5 minutes more. Season with salt and pepper.

Remove the pan from the heat. If the dip is a bit dry, add a couple of teaspoons of water to moisten. Alternatively, for a chunkier texture, leave the mixture as it is.

Let cool. Sprinkle with cilantro, if using, and serve with your choice of vegetable crudités and strips of pita bread.

avocado salsa

Serve this salsa as a dip with crudités, toasted pita bread, or chips—it's much better than any guacamole you can buy ready-made. To check whether the avocado is ripe, take the fruit in your hand and press gently at the neck end—if it is in peak condition, it will give a little without being too soft.

serves 4–6

2 ripe avocados, peeled, pitted, and diced

1 garlic clove, crushed

1 large red chile, seeded and finely chopped

2 tomatoes, seeded and diced

2 tablespoons olive oil

2 tablespoons freshly chopped cilantro

juice of ½ lime

salt and black pepper

Combine all the ingredients in a bowl and season to taste. Cover and set aside to infuse for 15 minutes, then serve immediately as the salsa will start to discolor after 30 minutes.

chile and mint raita

a large handful of mint

1 teaspoon salt

½ teaspoon sugar

1 cup plain yogurt

1 green chile, finely sliced
(optional)

serves
2–3

Q

Yogurt and mint are a common combination in India, often used to temper hot, spicy dishes. But with its own chile kick (optional) and some warm naan bread, this makes a great dip.

Very finely chop the mint leaves and put in a bowl with the salt, sugar, and yogurt and mix well. Serve sprinkled with the sliced green chile, if using, and some warm naan bread.

tomato, onion, and chile raita

1 cup plain yogurt

1 teaspoon salt

1 teaspoon sugar

juice of ½ lemon

1 red onion, finely diced

1 tomato, seeded and
chopped

2 inches cucumber, seeded
and chopped

1 red chile, chopped

1 green chile, chopped

serves
2–3

This combination of tomato, onion, and chile makes a great salsa by itself, but when mixed with yogurt, it's creamy and delicious. Serve with warm naan bread.

Put the yogurt, salt, sugar, and lemon juice in a bowl and mix to dissolve the sugar. Add the onion, tomato, cucumber, and chiles and stir gently. Refrigerate for 30 minutes, then serve with some warn naan bread.

cucumber and ginger raita

1 cup plain yogurt

1 inch fresh ginger, peeled
and grated

1 teaspoon salt

1 tablespoon sugar

1 tablespoon lemon juice

½ teaspoon ground turmeric

2 inches cucumber

serves
2–3

Serve this raita with a hot curry—cucumber and yogurt are known to help cool the effect of chiles.

Put the yogurt, ginger, salt, sugar, lemon juice, and turmeric into a bowl and mix to dissolve the sugar.

Cut the cucumber in half lengthwise and scrape out the seeds with a teaspoon. If the skin is tough or waxed, peel it off: otherwise leave it on. Cut the cucumber into matchstick strips, put into a bowl, and pour over the yogurt dressing. Refrigerate for 30 minutes, then serve.

Note See bottom picture on page 17 for photograph of all three raitas.

baba ganoush

Baba ganoush is a famous Middle-Eastern creamy eggplant purée with smoky overtones. Serve it as a dip or as a side dish.

 serves **8**

 Q

3 eggplants

¼ cup plain yogurt

2 tablespoons tahini (sesame seed paste)

1 garlic clove, crushed

1 teaspoon salt

juice of 1–2 lemons, to taste

1 tablespoon freshly chopped parsley (optional)

Using a pair of heatproof tongs, very carefully hold the eggplants over the open gas flame on top of the stove and cook until well charred on all sides. The steam created inside the vegetable will cook the flesh. The eggplants must be charred all over and soft in the middle. Remove from the flame and leave on a plate until cool enough to handle.

Carefully pull off the skins and stems. Don't leave any charred bits. Put the flesh into a bowl, then mash with a potato masher: the texture should not be too smooth. Add the yogurt, tahini, garlic, and salt and mash again.

Add the juice of 1 lemon, taste, then gradually add more juice until you achieve flavor and texture to your taste. Transfer to a bowl and sprinkle with parsley, if using. Serve with wedges of toasted pita bread.

*portobello mushrooms
with lemon and olive oil*

portobello *mushrooms* with *lemon* and *olive oil*

The earthy, almost meaty flavor of portobello mushrooms needs very little to improve it. Serve this as a simple, but tasty, snack when friends are round and complaining about being hungry.

To make the marinade, put the olive oil, soy sauce, lemon peel and juice, garlic, rosemary, and some pepper in a bowl, mix well, then pour over the mushrooms so that they are well covered. Set aside to infuse for 30 minutes.

Put a grill pan or skillet over medium heat to preheat. Put the mushrooms in the pan and cook for 5 minutes on each side or until softened.

Serve the mushrooms on top of a thick slice of toast and pour any remaining marinade juices over the top.

serves
4

4 large portobello mushrooms, about 8 oz.

Marinade

2 tablespoons olive oil

1 tablespoon soy sauce

grated peel and juice of 1 lemon

2 garlic cloves, crushed

4 sprigs of rosemary

black pepper

olive oil and *garlic* bread

This is a dairy-free version of everyone's guilty pleasure: garlic bread. Use sea salt flakes if you can, as they add texture. If you only have fine salt, reduce the quantity to ¼ teaspoon.

Preheat the oven to 400°F.

Slice the baguette on the diagonal at 1-inch intervals, but do not cut all the way through to the base. Put on a long piece of aluminum foil.

In a small bowl, combine the oil, garlic, and salt. Using a spoon, drizzle a little of the garlic oil between each slice of baguette, then brush the remaining garlic oil over the top. Wrap in the foil.

Bake in the preheated oven for 10 minutes until hot through. Serve the bread immediately.

serves
6–8

Q

1 baguette (French stick)

¼ cup olive oil

4 garlic cloves, crushed

½ teaspoon sea salt flakes

minty grilled *zucchini*

4 zucchini, about 2 lbs.

2 tablespoons olive oil

4 teaspoons white wine vinegar

a handful of mint, leaves torn

salt and black pepper

serves 4

Perfect for the summer, this Mediterranean recipe and simple char-grilling technique bring out the best in zucchini. Serve as a side dish or as a light lunch with another salad.

Trim and discard the ends of the zucchini, then cut the vegetable lengthwise into ribbonlike slices and put in a bowl. Drizzle with the olive oil and, using your hands, gently toss the slices until well coated.

Preheat a grill pan or nonstick skillet over high heat until very hot. Add the zucchini ribbons (in batches, if necessary) and cook until softened and marked with black stripes on both sides. Transfer to a shallow dish and drizzle with the vinegar while the zucchini are still warm. Add salt and pepper and let cool.

Pile the zucchini ribbons into a bowl, sprinkle with the mint, and add lots more black pepper. Serve immediately.

scrambled *eggs* with *mushrooms*

8 oz. portobello mushrooms, or mixed wild mushrooms

6 eggs

4 tablespoons butter

2 teaspoons freshly chopped thyme

salt and black pepper

serves 2

Add some sautéed mushrooms to scrambled eggs on toast and you've got yourself the perfect no-fuss snack for two, no matter what time of day it is.

Wipe the mushrooms with a damp cloth and cut into thick slices. Put the eggs in a bowl, add salt and pepper, and whisk until blended.

Melt 3 tablespoons of the butter in a large skillet. As soon as it stops foaming, add the mushrooms, thyme, salt, and pepper. Fry over medium heat until lightly browned and the juices are starting to run.

Push the mushrooms to one side of the skillet, add the remaining butter, then pour in the beaten eggs, stirring with a fork until almost set.

Gradually stir in the mushrooms from the sides of the skillet, cook a moment longer, and spoon onto toast to serve.

minty grilled zucchini

beefsteak tomatoes with garlic and herb butter

baked fennel with shallots and spicy dressing

beefsteak tomatoes with *garlic* and *herb* butter

serves 4

4 beefsteak tomatoes

3 garlic cloves, crushed

7 tablespoons butter, softened

1 teaspoon chili oil (optional)

a large handful of parsley, freshly chopped

black pepper

olive oil, for sprinkling

These are so easy to make, but beware that they need over an hour in the oven to bake to perfection. They would make a good, stress-free side dish for a special dinner, but they're also a great choice for an everyday meal for two.

Preheat the oven to 300°F.

Remove the stalk from each tomato and carefully cut out a small cavity for the filling.

Put the garlic, butter, chili oil, if using, parsley, and some pepper in a bowl and mix well. Fill the tomato cavities with the garlic mixture, pressing down gently as you go. Put on a baking sheet, sprinkle with olive oil, and roast in the preheated oven for 1 hour 20 minutes.

Eat hot from the oven with some of the cooking juices poured over the top.

baked *fennel* with *shallots* and spicy dressing

Fennel is a fantastic vegetable to have in your cooking repertoire because it's so versatile. You can roast it with other vegetables or serve it raw in a salad, thinly sliced or chopped. This is the kind of recipe that could serve up to 8 people as a small side, or far fewer as the main component of a meal.

serves 6–8

- 2 fennel bulbs
- 4 shallots, chopped
- 1 teaspoon sugar
- 3 tablespoons olive oil
- 1 garlic clove, crushed
- 1 inch fresh ginger, peeled and chopped
- a bunch of scallions, sliced
- 1 tablespoon sesame oil
- juice of 1 lemon
- ½ teaspoon chili powder
- salt and black pepper

Preheat the oven to 325°F.

Cut the base off the fennel bulbs and trim the tops. Cut each bulb lengthwise into 4 and cut out the hard core. Put in an ovenproof dish and add the shallots, sugar, and 2 tablespoons of the olive oil. Mix well and bake in the preheated oven for 30 minutes.

Put the remaining olive oil in a small saucepan, add the garlic and ginger, and cook over very low heat for 10 minutes. Add the scallions, sesame oil, lemon juice, chili powder, and salt and pepper to taste. Gently bring to a simmer, then pour over the roasted fennel. Mix and serve with the juices.

mozzarella and *basil* toasties

These cheesy snacks are great with beer or a glass of white wine if you've got friends over for the evening.

makes 16

Q

- 8 thin slices of white bread
- 7 oz. mozzarella
- a handful of basil, leaves torn
- ¼ cup olive oil
- salt and black pepper

Trim any thick crusts off the bread. Lay 4 slices of the bread on a work surface and divide the mozzarella and basil on top. Top each with a slice of bread.

Preheat a large, nonstick skillet over medium heat and add half of the olive oil. Sit the sandwiches in the skillet and drizzle the remaining oil on the top slices of bread.

Cook for 2–3 minutes, using a spatula to gently press down on the sandwiches. Turn over and cook for a further 2 minutes. Transfer to a cutting board and cut each sandwich into 4 fingers. Season with a little salt and pepper and serve immediately while the mozzarella is still molten.

whole cauliflower with olives

whole *cauliflower* with *olives*

This is such an impressive way to serve a whole creamy head of cauliflower—let your friends help themselves, pulling out the florets. It would complement a risotto nicely.

serves
4

1 large whole cauliflower, green leaves removed and reserved

2 onions, finely chopped

1¼ cups small, pitted green olives, sliced

⅓ cup olive oil, plus extra to serve

a handful of parsley, freshly chopped, to serve

salt

Line a large, heavy-based saucepan with the reserved outer leaves from the cauliflower. Put the cauliflower on top. Sprinkle with the onion, olives, and some salt, then pour over the olive oil. Cover with a lid, set over the lowest heat, and cook gently for about 40 minutes or until tender—there should be no resistance when a fork is inserted into the middle of the cauliflower.

Carefully lift the cauliflower out of the saucepan and onto a large plate—be very careful not to break it. Pile the onion and olives on top, then sprinkle with the parsley and more olive oil and serve.

creamy *spinach*

Steamed spinach is fine when you need a quick side vegetable - but try this creamy spinach for something a bit more special.

serves
4

Q

1 lb. fresh spinach

2 tablespoons cream

grated nutmeg (optional)

Discard any hard central stalks from the spinach and wash the leaves thoroughly in plenty of cold water. Drain well, then put the spinach in a large saucepan with only the water left clinging to the leaves. Cook for 2–3 minutes until wilted. Drain well, squeezing out any excess water. Chop finely.

Return the spinach to the rinsed pan and add 1 teaspoon water and the cream. Heat over medium heat for 1 minute, stirring. Serve immediately, sprinkled with a little grated nutmeg, if using.

smashed roast *potatoes*

serves 4

16 small new potatoes

2 tablespoons olive oil

1 teaspoon salt

1–2 sprigs of rosemary (optional)

You will need tiny little new potatoes to make perfect smashed roast spuds. The initial blast of a really hot oven is what makes the potatoes so soft and fluffy on the inside and about to burst out of their crispy little skins. This is a novel and highly effective way to roast potatoes so be warned, it's likely you may not go back to the old way of roasting after you try this!

Preheat the oven to 450°F and put a nonstick (if possible) roasting pan in the oven to heat up for 10 minutes.

Put the potatoes in a bowl with 1 tablespoon of the oil and toss to coat in the oil. Put the potatoes in the hot pan and roast in the preheated oven for 20 minutes.

Remove the roasting pan from the oven and turn the potatoes over. Gently press down on each potato with the back of large metal spoon until you hear the potato skin pop.

Drizzle the remaining oil over the potatoes, sprinkle with the salt, and throw in the rosemary, if using. Return to the oven for a further 10 minutes, until the potatoes are crispy and golden.

lemon roast *potato* wedges

serves 4

4 potatoes, each cut into 8 wedges

juice of ½ lemon

1–2 tablespoons olive oil

salt and black pepper

Your own homemade chunky fries. Serve with a veggie burger, like one of the options on pages 155–159.

Preheat the oven to 425°F.

Put the potato wedges in a nonstick (if possible) roasting pan, add the lemon juice, and season with salt and pepper. Drizzle with the olive oil and stir well. Cook in the preheated oven for 20–30 minutes until crisp and golden, turning once or twice. Transfer to a serving dish and serve.

Variation When the potatoes are ready, add 1 pint cherry tomatoes pricked with the point of a knife, then stir into the potatoes and return to the oven for 5 minutes or until the tomato skins start to split.

smashed roast potatoes

portuguese potatoes

portuguese *potatoes*

These are very similar to the Smashed Roast Potatoes on page 30, but they are cooked on the stove instead of in the oven, and they contain a generous amount of garlic—so these are only for very keen garlic lovers!

serves
6

¼ cup olive oil

3 lbs. small waxy new potatoes

6 garlic cloves, crushed

3 sprigs of rosemary

2 teaspoons sea salt flakes (or fine sea salt)

Heat the oil in a large, heavy-based saucepan set over medium heat. Add the potatoes. Add the garlic to the oil and potatoes along with the rosemary and salt. Stir well, reduce the heat to low, then cover and cook for 50–60 minutes for walnut-size potatoes or 1–1¼ hours for egg-size ones, stirring occasionally.

Note These Portuguese-style potatoes are also delicious as a cold side dish. You can make them the day before, and once cool, cover and refrigerate. Bring back to room temperature for 1 hour before serving.

crushed *peas*

Peas are always a great standby side dish because you're bound to have a bag in the freezer! They also have the added bonus of being delicious and making a good accompaniment to most food.

serves
3

Q

1 tablespoon olive oil

½ onion, thinly sliced

2 sage leaves

a small bunch of celery tops (optional—if you happen to have some celery in the fridge already)

10 oz. frozen peas

2 tablespoons light cream

salt and black pepper

kitchen twine

Heat the oil in a saucepan over medium heat. Add the onion and cook gently for 5 minutes, stirring frequently.

Tie together the sage leaves and celery tops, if using, with a piece of kitchen twine (for easy removal) and add to the onion along with the peas. Stir, cover, and cook for 10 minutes, stirring occasionally.

Uncover, stir through the cream, and heat through. Take off the heat and, using a potato masher, gently mash the peas until just crushed—they should retain some texture. Season to taste with salt and pepper and serve immediately.

roast *butternut squash*

makes 4–8

1 large butternut squash
or 2 small ones

2 tablespoons olive oil

6 tablespoons unsalted butter

a few sprigs of thyme

2 garlic cloves, sliced

salt and black pepper

Arguably the best-tasting squash and deep gold when roasted, butternut squash is an ideal accompaniment to so many dishes. If you roast it at a high heat, it will brown like a potato, or when cooked more gently, it marries well with fresh herbs.

Preheat the oven to 375°F.

Cut the squash in half lengthwise and scoop out the seeds and pith with a spoon. Cut each half into 3–4 wedges, according to the size of the squash. There is no need to peel them.

Put the oil and butter in a roasting pan and heat on top of the stove until melted. Add the wedges of butternut squash and baste the pieces, turning them carefully to cover. Push the sprigs of thyme and slices of garlic between the wedges and sprinkle with salt and pepper.

Roast in the preheated oven for 30 minutes, turning the pieces over a couple of times to brown them lightly as they finish cooking.

sweet potato skewers

serves 6

6 smallish sweet potatoes

3 tablespoons butter, melted

salt and black pepper

6 metal skewers

These potatoes are skewered through the center, then cut around to free each slice, leaving the skewer in place. This browns the slices individually without letting them fall to pieces. They are really good at picking up flavors from whatever else is in the pan, so bake them with a nut roast or similar.

Preheat the oven to 425°F.

Peel the sweet potatoes and skewer each one lengthwise through the center. Slice them around the skewer and separate the rounds.

Arrange them around a nut roast (or alone) in a roasting pan, baste generously with the melted butter, and season lightly with salt and pepper.

Roast in the preheated oven for 45 minutes or until browned—continue to baste them from time to time to prevent them from drying out.

roast butternut squash

1 tablespoon sunflower oil

1 lb. sugar snap peas

2 teaspoons sesame seeds

2 teaspoons sesame oil

sesame sugar snap peas

serves **4**

Q

These are the perfect accompaniment to a stir-fry or some simple fried tofu.

Heat a wok or skillet over high heat until hot, then add the sunflower oil. When the oil is hot, add the sugar snap peas. Stir-fry for about 4 minutes, stirring continuously, until tender. Add the sesame seeds and oil and stir-fry for 1 minute more. Serve immediately.

homemade baked *beans*

4 x 15-oz. cans white beans, such as navy, cannellini, or borlotti, rinsed and drained

3 onions, finely chopped

4 garlic cloves, crushed

2 tablespoons olive oil

1–1½ teaspoons paprika

1½–2 tablespoons molasses

3 tablespoons tomato paste

4 teaspoons Worcestershire sauce (optional)

2 cups boiling water

salt and black pepper

serves **15!**

Ready-prepared baked beans are so cheap to buy that it may seem like madness to make your own but most commercially prepared versions are extremely high in salt and sugar. This may seem like a large quantity to make, but the beans freeze well. To freeze, let cool, then transfer to freezerproof containers. Freeze for up to 1 month. Serve the traditional way, on yummy buttered toast, or on a baked sweet potato.

Preheat the oven to 350°F.

Put the beans in a large casserole dish or Dutch oven, add all the remaining ingredients, and season lightly with salt and pepper. Mix well.

Cover and cook in the preheated oven for 1–1¼ hours, stirring occasionally, until the sauce is thick and rich in taste and texture. Check the seasoning; add extra Worcestershire sauce, if necessary, and extra molasses if still slightly bitter.

*chile greens
with garlic crisps*

chile *greens* with *garlic* crisps

The word "greens"—used to describe any leafy green—includes Swiss chard, bok choy, spinach, and more. Many need only brief cooking—steam or stir-fry to retain color, nutrients, and flavor. Remove any tough stalks before cooking.

serves
4

Q

1 lb. greens (see Introduction, left)

2 tablespoons olive oil

4 garlic cloves, sliced

1 red chile, seeded and thinly sliced

salt and black pepper

Chop the greens (if using bok choy, cut lengthwise into wedges). Heat the olive oil in a large saucepan. Add the garlic, fry until golden and crisp, about 2–3 minutes, then remove and set aside. Add the chile to the infused oil in the pan and cook for 1 minute. Tip in the greens—they will splutter, so stand back. Add salt and pepper and mix well. Cover and cook, turning occasionally using tongs, until tender: Swiss chard and bok choy about 3 minutes; spinach, about 1–2 minutes.

Transfer to a dish and top with the garlic crisps to serve.

salads

*tabbouleh with chickpeas
and spring salad*

tabbouleh with *chickpeas* and *spring salad*

When buying salad greens, keep in mind you will need about two large handfuls per person. The fresh ingredients are combined here with bulgur wheat, a nutty grain that is more nutritious than rice or couscous. Simply cover with boiling water to soften and add to your favorite salad ingredients.

Put the bulgur wheat in a heatproof bowl and pour over the boiling water. Stir once, cover tightly with plastic wrap, and set aside for 8–10 minutes.

Put the lemon juice and olive oil in a small bowl and whisk. Pour over the bulgur wheat and stir well with a fork, fluffing up the bulgur and separating the grains.

Put the bulgur wheat in a large bowl with the parsley, mint, tomatoes, chickpeas, and salad greens. Use your hands to toss everything together. Season well with salt and black pepper.

serves
4

Q

½ cup fine bulgur wheat

½ cup boiling water

2 tablespoons lemon juice

¼ cup olive oil

a small handful of parsley, freshly chopped

a large handful of mint, freshly chopped

1 pint of cherry tomatoes, halved

14-oz. can chickpeas, rinsed and drained

4–5 oz. spring salad mix

salt and black pepper

black bean and *avocado* salad

The combination of colors and textures in this salad is a knockout. It can be made with other beans, but black beans work particularly well, as they highlight the colors of the other ingredients.

Put the beans in a large salad bowl and add the corn, bell pepper, herbs, and olive oil. Stir well and cover until required.

When ready to serve, peel and pit the avocado, then cut into small cubes and put in a small bowl. Add the lemon juice, season with salt and pepper, and mix well. Add the avocado to the bean salad and mix well. Taste and add more salt and pepper, if necessary, then serve.

serves
4

Q

2 x 14-oz. cans black beans, drained

14 oz. canned corn kernels, drained

1 large red bell pepper, seeded and diced

a handful of parsley, freshly chopped

a handful of basil, freshly chopped

3 tablespoons olive oil

1 avocado

1 tablespoon lemon juice

salt and black pepper

½ cup bulgur wheat

2 scallions, chopped

1 celery rib, finely chopped

1 red bell pepper, seeded and finely chopped

1 green apple, cored and chopped

Dressing

1 tablespoon grainy mustard

1 tablespoon honey

2 tablespoons cider or white wine vinegar

2 tablespoons mayonnaise

a handful of parsley, freshly chopped

black pepper

5 oz. feta, cubed

1 garlic clove, crushed

2 tablespoons freshly chopped dill

2 tablespoons freshly chopped mint

4 tablespoons olive oil

grated peel of 1 lemon and juice of ½ lemon

1 small, crisp lettuce, chopped

6 oz. tomatoes, chopped

4 inches cucumber, chopped

2 oz. pitted black olives

1 small red onion, chopped

1 ripe avocado, peeled, pitted, and chopped

black pepper

apple and *bulgur wheat* salad

 serves 4–6

Bulgur wheat-based salads such as tabbouleh are quick, easy, and substantial. You could also substitute another grain, such as barley, cooked according to the package instructions.

Put the bulgur wheat in a bowl and cover with cold water. Let soak for 30 minutes until tender but not too soft. Drain well and press down hard on the bulgur wheat with the back of a spoon to squeeze out excess water.

Put the bulgur wheat in a salad bowl with the scallions, celery, bell pepper, and apple.

To make the dressing, whisk together the mustard, honey, vinegar, and mayonnaise in a small bowl and add black pepper to taste. Add this to the bulgur mixture, cover, and refrigerate until needed.

Remove the salad from the refrigerator about 30 minutes before serving and bring to room temperature. Stir in the chopped parsley to serve.

lemon and *herb feta* salad

 serves 2

 Q

Marinate the cheese for as long as you like—it will keep in the fridge overnight. Keep the tomatoes out of the fridge as they taste much better and sweeter at room temperature; also make sure you choose ripe tomatoes and ripe, ready-to-eat avocado.

Put the feta cubes in a shallow bowl. In another small bowl mix together the garlic, herbs, olive oil, lemon peel, and lemon juice. Season the dressing with pepper and pour over the feta. Cover and let marinate for a few minutes in a cool place, or in a refrigerator for longer.

Arrange the salad leaves in 2 bowls. Put the tomatoes, cucumber, olives, onion, and avocado on the top, then spoon the marinated feta over the salad. Drizzle any remaining dressing over the salad and serve.

*apple and bulgur
wheat salad*

classic italian salad

classic italian salad

If you ask for a mixed salad in Italy, this is what you will get. It's ultra simple but sometimes, on a warm summer's day, that's exactly what you want from a salad.

serves
4

Q

Bring a large saucepan of salted water to a boil, add the potatoes, bring back to a boil, and simmer for about 15 minutes or until tender. Add the green beans to the pan 4 minutes before the potatoes are cooked. Drain and cover with cold water to stop the vegetables cooking further. When cold, drain well.

Remove the beans to a bowl, slice the potatoes thickly, and add to the beans. Add the olive oil and olives and toss well.

Add the lettuce to the potatoes along with the tomatoes. Toss lightly. Transfer to a serving bowl and sprinkle with parsley. Serve with olive oil, vinegar, and salt and pepper so the salad can be dressed at the table.

12 oz. waxy potatoes, peeled

6 oz. green beans, trimmed

1 tablespoon olive oil, plus extra to serve

2 oz. pitted black or green olives

1 small crisp lettuce, torn into bite-size pieces

2 large ripe tomatoes, quartered

3 tablespoons freshly chopped parsley

salt and black pepper

red wine vinegar, to serve

avocado and *chickpea* salad

This is a fresh and yet instant meal for lazy evenings. Although it's just a salad, it's got eggs, chickpeas, and avocados—so it's nice and filling, and ideal with a chunk of bread on the side.

serves
4

Q

Put the eggs in a small saucepan of water, bring to a boil, and cook until hard-boiled, 8–9 minutes. Drain, cool, shell, cut into quarters, and set aside.

To make the dressing, put the lemon juice in a bowl with the milk, fromage frais or yogurt, and snipped chives. Season generously with salt and pepper and stir until smooth.

Put the spinach, chickpeas, avocados, and eggs in a bowl. Sprinkle with the paprika, then spoon over the dressing.

2 eggs

8 oz. baby spinach

14-oz. can chickpeas, rinsed and drained

2 ripe avocados, peeled, pitted, and chopped

2 teaspoons sweet paprika

Dressing

juice of 1 lemon

3 tablespoons milk

2 tablespoons fromage frais or thick yogurt

a bunch of chives, snipped

salt and black pepper

1 lb. red cabbage, shredded

3 tablespoons red or white wine vinegar

1 lb. white cabbage, shredded

1 cup grated carrot

1 large Granny Smith apple, peeled, cored, and grated

¼ cup pumpkin seeds, toasted

salt and black pepper

Dressing

juice of ½ orange

1 tablespoon white wine vinegar

1 teaspoon sugar

1 tablespoon vegetable oil

¾ cup plain yogurt

¾ cup crème fraîche or sour cream

apple cole slaw

serves 6–8

Plastic tubs of cole slaw are really no match for the real thing and, if you like it but have never made it yourself, you should try this recipe with its light creamy dressing and healthy apple.

Put the red cabbage in a heatproof bowl. Heat the wine vinegar in a small saucepan until just boiling. Stir in a pinch of salt, then pour the mixture over the red cabbage. Toss well. This helps to set the color.

In a serving bowl, combine the red cabbage, white cabbage, carrot, and apple and toss well to combine.

To make the dressing, put the orange juice, vinegar, salt, and sugar in a small bowl and use a fork or small whisk to mix. Add the oil, yogurt, and crème fraîche or sour cream. Mix well and season to taste with pepper.

Pour the dressing over the cabbage mixture and toss well. Taste for seasoning and adjust if necessary—it may need more salt, or more vinegar. Refrigerate for several hours before serving. When ready to serve, sprinkle with toasted pumpkin seeds. This is best eaten on the day it is prepared.

thai cole slaw

serves 4

This hybrid Thai cole slaw is based on the classic "som tum," usually made from grated green papaya but replaced here with red cabbage. This recipe is a merging of these two classic dishes with a delicious new twist.

4 oz. green beans, trimmed

2 cups shredded red or white cabbage

3 tomatoes, seeded and sliced

4 scallions, sliced

⅓ cup roasted peanuts, chopped

Dressing

a handful of cilantro

2 red chiles, seeded

2 garlic cloves, chopped

2 tablespoons light soy sauce

2 tablespoons lime juice

2 tablespoons brown sugar

To make the dressing, reserve a few cilantro leaves, then very finely chop the rest. Very finely chop the chiles and add to the chopped cilantro with the garlic, soy sauce, lime juice, and sugar and mix well. Set aside.

Blanch the beans in boiling water for 2 minutes. Drain and cover with cold water to stop them cooking further. When cold, drain well. Mix the cabbage, beans, tomatoes, and scallions in a bowl. Pour the dressing on top, toss well to coat, and marinate for about 30 minutes. Spoon into bowls, sprinkle with the peanuts, and the reserved cilantro leaves, then serve.

apple cole slaw

tomato, mozzarella,
and basil salad

tomato, mozzarella, and *basil* salad

serves
4

Q

2 balls of buffalo mozzarella,
5 oz. each

2 large ripe tomatoes, roughly
the same size as the balls
of mozzarella

2 oz. basil leaves

about ½ cup olive oil

salt and black pepper

This classic salad born on the Isle of Capri is hard to beat. It combines three ingredients that work totally in harmony with each other—mozzarella, tomato, and basil. Sliced avocado is also a delicious addition (although not traditional). This is the kind of super easy—but quite smart—dish you want to throw together when friends are over for dinner.

Cut the mozzarella and tomatoes into slices about ¼ inch thick. Arrange the tomato slices on a large plate and season with salt and pepper. Put 1 slice of mozzarella on each slice of tomato and top with a basil leaf. Tear up the remaining basil and scatter over the top. Drizzle with a generous amount of olive oil just before serving.

This salad must be made at the last moment to prevent the tomatoes from weeping and the mozzarella from drying out. Serve at room temperature, never chilled, as this would kill the flavors.

Variation If using avocado, halve and peel one ripe avocado, remove the pit, and slice the flesh. Intersperse the slices of avocado with the tomato and mozzarella.

grated *cucumber, sour cream,* and *paprika* salad

This is strictly speaking a salad, but it works well on a baked potato. For meat-eating friends, serve it with cold chicken.

serves
4

Wash the cucumbers in warm soapy water to remove any wax or residues. Rinse and dry well. Grate them on the rough side of a cheese grater—it shouldn't be too fine. Transfer to a strainer or colander set over a plate, sprinkle with salt, and mix well. Let drain for 30 minutes.

Rinse the grated cucumber under cold running water, pat dry with a clean kitchen towel, then transfer to a bowl. Add the scallions and vinegar and mix with a fork. Season well with salt and pepper. Spread the cucumber mixture in an even layer on a serving plate.

Season the sour cream with salt, pepper, and a pinch of paprika, then spoon it over the top of the cucumber mixture. Sprinkle liberally with the remaining paprika and serve immediately.

2 large cucumbers

a bunch of scallions, trimmed and very finely shredded or 1 small red onion, very finely chopped

2 teaspoons white wine vinegar

6 tablespoons sour cream

2 teaspoons sweet paprika

salt and black pepper

feta salad with *sugar snap peas*

The heat of the chile, the cool of the yogurt and cucumber together with the saltiness of the feta make this refreshing salad just perfect for summer lunches.

serves
4

Q

Blanch the sugar snap peas in boiling water for 30 seconds. Drain and cover with cold water to stop them cooking further. When cold, drain well.

Cook the beans in boiling water for 4 minutes. Drain and cover with cold water to stop them cooking further. When cold, drain well.

To make the dressing, put the yogurt, olive oil, and lemon juice in a small bowl and whisk well.

Put the feta in a large bowl, add the sugar snaps, beans, cucumber, and mint. Pour the dressing over the salad, toss well, then serve topped with the chile, if using.

6 oz. sugar snap peas

8 oz. green beans, trimmed

8 oz. feta, cubed

½ cucumber, seeded and chopped

a handful of mint, freshly chopped

1 red chile, seeded and finely chopped (optional)

salt

Dressing

3 tablespoons Greek yogurt

1 tablespoon olive oil

1 tablespoon lemon juice

tomato and *bread* salad

serves 4–6

2 red bell peppers, halved and seeded

2 yellow bell peppers, halved and seeded

1 lb. ripe tomatoes

¼ cup red wine vinegar

2 garlic cloves, crushed

½ cup olive oil, plus extra for drizzling

2 tablespoons capers

⅓ cup pitted black olives

1 small or ½ large ciabatta or other white loaf, cubed

a bunch of basil, leaves torn

black pepper

This is an ingenious Italian peasant salad designed to make good use of very ripe tomatoes and stale (but not moldy!) bread. The bread drinks up the rich flavors of the tomato and roasted bell pepper dressing. It's important to use a crusty, firm-crumbed bread so it doesn't revert to a soggy, dough-like state.

Preheat the broiler to high.

Put the bell peppers cut-side down on a baking sheet and broil until blistered and charred. Transfer to a plastic bag, seal, and let cool (the steam will loosen the skin, making it easier to peel). Scrape off and discard the skin, then cut the peppers into strips, reserving any juice.

Halve the tomatoes and scoop out the cores and seeds over a bowl to catch the juice. Purée the cores and seeds in a blender, then press the extra juice through a strainer into the bowl. Discard the pulp and seeds. Cut the tomato halves into strips.

Put the tomato juice, vinegar, garlic, and some black pepper in a bowl. Gradually add the olive oil, whisking until blended.

Mix the strips of peppers and tomatoes in a bowl, add the capers, olives, ciabatta, and basil and mix. Add the dressing, toss well to coat, then set aside for 1 hour to infuse. Drizzle with olive oil and serve.

tomato, avocado, and lime salad with crisp tortillas

tomato, avocado, and *lime* salad with crisp *tortillas*

This salad makes a tasty addition to a Mexican dish. The crisp tortillas are a great idea as they give the dish an extra bite.

serves
6

Q

Put the lime juice in a bowl. Cut the avocados in half, remove the pits, and peel. Cut each half into 4 wedges and toss with the lime juice.

Using a small knife, cut the top and bottom off of the lime. Cut away the skin and pith. Carefully slice between each segment and remove the flesh. Combine the lime flesh with the avocados and add the cilantro, tomatoes, and ¼ cup of the oil. Season with salt and pepper and set aside.

Preheat the broiler to hot.

In a small bowl, combine the garlic and the remaining oil. Brush the oil and garlic mixture over the tortillas and broil for about 1 minute until brown. Break the toasted tortillas into pieces and scatter over the salad.

juice of 1 lime, plus 1 lime

4 ripe, firm avocados

a handful of cilantro, freshly chopped

24 cherry tomatoes, halved

⅓ cup olive oil

2 garlic cloves, crushed

2 flour tortillas

salt and black pepper

lebanese *halloumi* salad

serves 2

Q

1 large whole-wheat pita bread, opened out

1 small cucumber, seeded and cut into chunks

2 large vine-ripened tomatoes, seeded and cut into chunks

1 small red bell pepper, seeded and sliced

10 pitted black olives, halved

½ small red onion, sliced

3 tablespoons freshly chopped parsley

3 tablespoons freshly chopped mint

5 oz. halloumi (patted dry with paper towels), cubed

Dressing

2 tablespoons olive oil, plus extra for frying

2 tablespoons lemon juice

½ teaspoon ground cumin (optional)

salt and black pepper

Fresh herbs add color, flavor, and nutritional value to this Lebanese salad, and although halloumi is not a traditional ingredient, the cheese adds valuable protein. This is a good get-ahead lunch—make some for your dinner one evening, then keep the leftovers for lunch the next day. If you do this, only add the pita just before serving so it remains crisp.

Preheat the broiler to medium.

Grill the pita bread until lightly golden and crisp. Let cool.

Meanwhile, mix together the oil, lemon juice, and cumin, if using, for the dressing. Season with salt and pepper.

Put the cucumber, tomatoes, and bell pepper in a serving bowl, then add the olives, onion, parsley, and mint. Pour the dressing over and toss until combined. Break the crisp pita into pieces and mix into the salad.

Heat a little oil in a skillet and fry the halloumi until it starts to color. Divide the salad between 2 plates, then top with the halloumi.

*garden salad with
garlic toasts*

garden salad with *garlic* toasts

The best thing about this salad is that you can use whatever salad greens you can find that look ultra crisp and fresh. These are then spruced up with cheat's croutons, chunks of cheese, and the best homemade salad cream you can imagine.

serves
4

Q

Preheat the broiler to medium.

To make the salad cream, put the salt, sugar, mustard, vinegar, and oil in a bowl and whisk to dissolve the salt and sugar. Begin to add the milk, very slowly at first and whisking the whole time. Continue to add all of the milk until you have a dressing the consistency of a thin custard.

Brush a little oil over each side of the bread slices. Lightly broil the bread until golden on both sides and rub the garlic cloves over the toast. Allow the toast to cool and crisp up.

Hard-boil the eggs following the instructions in the Avocado and Chickpea Salad recipe on page 45. Drain, cool, shell, cut into quarters, and combine with the remaining ingredients in a large bowl. Roughly break up the pieces of toast and add to the salad with some of the salad cream, then gently toss to combine. Serve immediately.

6 thin slices of bread

3–4 garlic cloves

2 eggs

3 large handfuls of salad, such as baby romaine, butterhead, and curly endive

3 ripe tomatoes

1 bunch of scallions

7 oz. cheddar

olive oil, for brushing

Salad cream

1 teaspoon salt

1 teaspoon sugar

1 tablespoon mild mustard

1 tablespoon white wine vinegar

¼ cup olive oil

⅛ cup milk

warm *potato* salad

This versatile salad can be eaten hot or cold, as a meal in itself or, for meat-eaters, as an accompaniment to broiled chicken.

serves
4

Boil the potatoes in a large saucepan of simmering water for 15–20 minutes until the potatoes are tender when pierced with a fork. Drain and let cool slightly. When cool enough to handle, cut them into 1-inch cubes and put in a serving bowl.

Hard-boil the eggs following the instructions in the Avocado and Chickpea Salad recipe on page 45. Drain, cool, shell, and chop.

Put the yogurt, crème fraîche or sour cream, and garlic in a separate bowl and mix. Spoon the mixture over the potatoes, add the cucumber, bell pepper, and eggs and stir carefully. Serve hot or cold.

1 lb. boiling potatoes, unpeeled

2 eggs

1 tablespoon plain yogurt

1 tablespoon crème fraîche or sour cream

1 garlic clove, crushed

½ cucumber, finely chopped

1 small red bell pepper, seeded and finely chopped

cauliflower and swiss chard salad with chickpeas

¼ cup olive oil

1 small head of cauliflower, separated into large florets

1 teaspoon ground cumin

6 Swiss chard leaves, cut into 1-inch-wide strips

1 red onion, cut into wedges

2 garlic cloves, chopped

14-oz. can chickpeas, rinsed and drained

¼ cup tahini (sesame seed paste)

2 tablespoons lemon juice

¼ teaspoon black pepper

salt

serves 4

Q

This is such a fantastic and unusual warm salad. It's light and slightly spicy, with a Middle-Eastern flavor.

Heat the oil in a skillet over high heat, add the cauliflower florets, and cook for 8–10 minutes, turning often, until they are a dark, golden brown. Add the cumin and cook, stirring, for 1 minute. Add the Swiss chard, onion, and garlic to the skillet and cook for a further 2–3 minutes. Add the chickpeas and stir. Season to taste with salt.

Combine the tahini, lemon juice, and pepper in a small bowl and add a little salt to taste. Whisk to combine. Transfer the vegetables to a bowl and drizzle the dressing over the top to serve.

warm puy lentil salad

1 cup cherry tomatoes

1½ cups Puy lentils or other brown lentils

grated peel and juice of 1 lemon

1 dried bay leaf

2 garlic cloves, chopped

2 red onions, diced

½ cup pitted green olives

a handful of parsley, freshly chopped

¼ cup olive oil, plus extra for frying

salt and black pepper

4 oz. Parmesan or mozzarella, to serve (optional)

serves 4

Really, this is a salad for all seasons. It works wonderfully served warm or cold and is bound to become a regular feature in your cooking repertoire.

Preheat the oven to 250°F.

Grease a baking sheet with olive or vegetable oil. Put the cherry tomatoes on the sheet and cook in the preheated oven for 40 minutes.

Meanwhile, put the lentils in a saucepan. Add the lemon peel and juice, bay leaf, garlic, and enough water to cover. Stir, bring to a boil, then simmer for about 40 minutes or until the lentils are soft.

Drain the lentils thoroughly and transfer to a large bowl. Add the tomatoes, red onion, olives, parsley, olive oil, salt, and pepper. Toss gently, then serve topped with slices of Parmesan or mozzarella, if using.

cauliflower and swiss chard
salad with chickpeas

warm chickpea salad with
spiced mushrooms

warm *chickpea* salad with spiced *mushrooms*

This entrée salad was inspired by Middle-Eastern cuisine, where beans, yogurt, and mint are widely used. Make this dish more substantial by serving it with couscous or bulgur wheat.

Heat 2 tablespoons of the oil in a skillet over medium heat. Add the mushrooms, season with salt, and cook until softened. Reduce the heat, then add the garlic, chile, and chickpeas. Fry for 2 minutes, then add the cumin and half the lemon juice. Cook until the juices in the skillet evaporate, then set aside.

Put the yogurt in a bowl, then add the chopped mint and the remaining lemon juice and oil. Add salt and pepper and mix until blended. Divide the spinach between 4 plates, add the chickpea and mushroom mixture, then pour the yogurt dressing over the top and serve.

serves 4

3 tablespoons olive oil

10 oz. button mushrooms

2 garlic cloves, chopped

1 red chile, seeded and chopped

14-oz. can chickpeas, rinsed and drained

2 teaspoons ground cumin

juice of 1 lemon

¾ cup Greek or thick plain yogurt

a large handful of mint, freshly chopped

8 oz. baby spinach

salt and black pepper

grilled *asparagus* and *leaf* salad with *sesame-soy* dressing

Pan-grilling is one of the best ways of cooking asparagus spears—it seals in their sweet, earthy flavor. Turn this salad into a main dish by adding boiled eggs.

Lightly toast the sesame seeds in a dry skillet, stirring frequently, until golden and popping. Transfer to a bowl and let cool.

Wash the asparagus and cut off any tough stalks. Brush with olive oil. Heat a stove-top grill pan or skillet until very hot. Add the asparagus (in batches, if necessary) and cook, turning occasionally, until bright green, blistered and slightly charred, about 5–7 minutes (depending on thickness).

Put the toasted sesame seeds, soy sauce, and balsamic vinegar in a bowl and gradually whisk in the oil until emulsified. To assemble, put the salad greens on a platter, arrange the asparagus on top, drizzle with the sesame dressing, and serve.

serves 2–3

2 tablespoons sesame seeds

a bunch of asparagus, about 12 spears

1 tablespoon dark soy sauce

1 tablespoon balsamic vinegar

3 tablespoons olive oil, plus extra for brushing

1 cup mixed salad greens, such as arugula, watercress, and spinach

warm *goat cheese* salad

serves **4**

Q

7 oz. mixed salad greens

12 oz. goat cheese with rind, cut into 4 rounds

2 avocados, peeled, pitted, and chopped

1 cup shelled pecans, toasted

salt and black pepper

Dressing

1 tablespoon sugar

1 teaspoon tomato paste

2 tablespoons balsamic vinegar

⅓ cup olive oil

2 ripe tomatoes, seeded and finely chopped

Nothing beats broiled goat cheese—warm, slightly caramelized, and oozingly good—especially served on a tasty salad.

To make the dressing, put the sugar and 1 tablespoon water into a heavy-based saucepan. Heat gently, whisking constantly until the sugar has dissolved. Transfer the sugar syrup to a bowl and add the tomato paste and balsamic vinegar, whisking rapidly until thoroughly combined. Add the olive oil slowly, whisking constantly until emulsified. Add the tomatoes and mix well. Set aside.

Divide the salad greens between 4 plates and season to taste with salt and pepper. Heat a large nonstick skillet over medium-high heat. Add the goat cheese slices and cook until they start to bubble and brown in places, about 5 minutes.

Arrange the avocados and pecans over the salad greens. Drizzle the dressing over the top. Lift a slice of goat cheese onto the center of each plate. Top with a little more dressing.

thrown-together *olives, tomatoes,* and *feta*

serves **4–6**

8 oz. tomatoes, halved

brown sugar, to taste

2 garlic cloves, thinly sliced

1 cup pitted green olives

1 cup pitted black olives

8 oz. feta, cubed

2 tablespoons chili oil (optional)

2 tablespoons olive oil

grated peel of ½ lemon

a handful of basil leaves

salt

This a popular tapas recipe in Spain. Eat it as a snack or as a little salad in itself. The recipe makes a generous amount so keep any leftovers in a covered bowl in the refrigerator to enjoy over several days.

Preheat the oven to 400°F.

Remove the hard core from the tomatoes by making a V-shaped incision with a sharp knife. Put the tomatoes on a baking sheet and sprinkle with salt and brown sugar. Push a slice of garlic into the soft seeds of each tomato, then roast in the preheated oven for 1 hour until quite dry.

Put the tomatoes in a serving bowl, add the olives, feta, chili oil, if using, olive oil, and lemon peel. Toss well, top with the basil, then serve.

warm goat cheese salad

pasta

*penne with
tomatoes and basil*

penne with tomatoes and basil

This pasta dish couldn't be simpler, but you do need to leave the garlic, olive oil, and basil to infuse the tomatoes for about an hour to become deliciously fragrant. The end result is a fabulous taste of Italy.

serves 4

14 oz. ripe cherry tomatoes, halved

2 garlic cloves, crushed

½ cup olive oil

a small handful of basil, leaves torn

14 oz. dried penne

salt and black pepper

Put the tomatoes and garlic in a large bowl. Pour over the olive oil. Season with salt and pepper, add half the basil, and leave for an hour or so to infuse. A warmish place is best, or at room temperature, but not the fridge because the cold will stop the oil from absorbing the flavors.

Bring a big saucepan of water to a boil and add a pinch of salt. Drop in the pasta and cook according to the instructions on the package.

Drain the pasta and add it to the bowl with the infused tomatoes. Toss well so that the oil coats all the pieces and finally stir in the remaining torn basil.

whole-wheat spaghetti with zucchini and herbs

The nutty taste of whole-wheat pasta works brilliantly here with the bright flavors of mint, chili, and lemon.

serves 4

Q

14 oz. dried whole-wheat spaghetti

¼ cup olive oil

6 zucchini, grated

2 red onions, finely chopped

2 garlic cloves, chopped

1 tablespoon lemon juice

½ teaspoon hot red pepper flakes

a large handful of mint, freshly chopped

a large handful of parsley, freshly chopped

grated Parmesan, to serve

salt

Bring a large saucepan of water to a boil and add a pinch of salt. Drop in the pasta and cook according to the instructions on the package.

Meanwhile, heat the olive oil in a large, heavy-based skillet over medium heat. Add the zucchini and onions and cook, stirring, for about 10 minutes, until softened and turning golden.

Add the garlic, lemon juice, and pepper flakes and cook for 1 minute further. Remove from the heat.

Drain the pasta and add to the skillet with the zucchini mixture. Add the herbs and toss well to combine. Serve immediately, sprinkled with some grated Parmesan.

farfalle with *zucchini, raisins,* and *pine nuts*

serves
4

2 tablespoons golden raisins

14 oz. dried farfalle

3 tablespoons olive oil

3 medium zucchini, thinly sliced

3 tablespoons pine nuts

2 garlic cloves, crushed

grated peel of 1 lemon

salt and black pepper

This is a lovely vegetarian pasta dish, but it's such a delicious mixture of flavors and textures that everyone seems to love it. Any short pasta shape would work nicely, so if you have a particular favorite, don't be afraid to try it.

Put the raisins into a little dish and cover them with hot water. Leave them for about 15 minutes, until they are nice and plump.

Bring a large saucepan of water to a boil and add a pinch of salt. Drop in the pasta and cook according to the instructions on the package.

Heat the olive oil in a large saucepan over medium heat and fry the zucchini for 6–8 minutes, until golden. Add the pine nuts and cook for a further 2–3 minutes, until the pine nuts are golden.

Add the garlic and cook for just 2 minutes; you don't want it to cook so much that it browns, which is when it becomes bitter.

Drain the raisins and stir them into the mixture together with the lemon peel. Season the mixture to taste with salt and pepper.

Drain the pasta and toss with the zucchini and raisin mixture.

pappardelle with *parsley*

serves
4

Q

14 oz. dried pappardelle

a bunch of parsley, freshly chopped

1 garlic clove, finely chopped

4 tablespoons olive oil

juice of ½ lemon

salt and black pepper

Pappardelle is like flat, wide spaghetti. Because of its extra width, whatever sauce you add, it will cling more easily and give more flavor. This is the kind of recipe you can turn to when your kitchen cupboards are looking totally bare.

Bring a large saucepan of water to a boil and add a pinch of salt. Drop in the pasta and cook according to the instructions on the package.

Drain the pasta and return it to the pan, off the heat. Add the parsley, garlic, oil, lemon juice, and salt and pepper to taste. Toss well, then serve.

farfalle with zucchini,
raisins, and pine nuts

spaghetti with butternut squash, sage, and pecorino

spaghetti with butternut squash, sage, and pecorino

This tasty pasta is inspired by the classic Italian dish of pumpkin-filled ravioli with sage butter except this is an inside-out version and therefore much easier to make.

Bring a large saucepan of water to a boil and add a pinch of salt. Drop in the pasta and cook according to the instructions on the package.

Heat the oil in a skillet over high heat. Add the squash and cook for 5–6 minutes, turning often, until golden but not breaking up. Add the garlic and sage to the skillet and cook for 2–3 minutes. Remove from the heat and let sit to allow the flavors to develop.

Drain the pasta well and return to the warm pan with the squash mixture. Add the parsley and half of the Pecorino and season well with salt and pepper. Serve with the remaining cheese sprinkled over the top.

serves 4

Q

14 oz. dried spaghetti

¼ cup olive oil

14 oz. butternut squash, peeled, seeded, and cut into thin wedges

2 garlic cloves, chopped

10–12 small sage leaves

a handful of parsley, freshly chopped

½ cup grated Pecorino (or shaved with a vegetable peeler)

salt and black pepper

spaghetti with herbs and garlic

If you like chiles, there is a similar dish to this that includes a couple of chopped chiles or a pinch of hot red pepper flakes with the garlic-infused olive oil. Never be afraid to experiment—that's how we discover new things!

Bring a large saucepan of water to a boil and add a pinch of salt. Drop in the pasta and cook according to the instructions on the package.

Heat the oil in a skillet over medium heat. Add the whole garlic cloves to the skillet and allow to warm and infuse the oil for 3–4 minutes.

Fish the garlic out of the oil with a slotted spoon and discard.

Drain the pasta and toss with the garlic-infused oil, the lemon peel, and the herbs. Serve at once with grated Parmesan.

serves 4

Q

14 oz. dried spaghetti

⅓ cup olive oil

3 garlic cloves, peeled but left whole

grated peel of 1 lemon

a large handful of mixed fresh herbs (such as chives, parsley, and basil), leaves torn

grated Parmesan, to serve

penne with *mozzarella, herbs, and tomatoes*

14 oz. dried penne

14-oz. can chopped tomatoes

1 small dried red chile

3–4 garlic cloves, chopped

1 onion, chopped

2 tablespoons tomato paste

leaves from 2 sprigs of oregano, marjoram, basil, or rosemary, freshly chopped

1 tablespoon sugar

2 tablespoons capers or pitted black olives, rinsed and drained (optional)

6 oz. mozzarella, thinly sliced

2 tablespoons olive oil

salt and black pepper

serves
4

Q

There's so much flavor packed into this dish that you'll come back to it time and time again when you don't know what to cook for your dinner. Use whichever fresh herbs you already have or can most easily find. Consider buying a jar of capers and keeping it on standby in the fridge for recipes such as this —capers always come in handy, and they are great at pepping up an otherwise bland dish.

Bring a large saucepan of water to a boil and add a pinch of salt. Drop in the pasta and cook according to the instructions on the package.

Put the tomatoes in a large, shallow saucepan or skillet. Add the chile, garlic, onion, tomato paste, oregano (or other herb), sugar, and capers or olives. Cook, stirring, over high heat until the sauce is thick and reduced to about half its original volume. Add salt and pepper to taste. Fish out the whole chile and discard.

Drain the pasta, reserving 3 tablespoons of the cooking liquid, then return the pasta and reserved liquid to the saucepan. Add the sliced mozzarella. Pour the hot sauce over the top and toss and stir until well mixed and the mozzarella is softened and melting. Drizzle with the olive oil and serve.

penne with mozzarella, herbs, and tomatoes

spaghetti with *peas* and *mint*

Try to use little French petits pois for this pasta dish instead of larger, more mature peas. They have a sweeter flavor and a satisfying pop when you bite into them. Buy them frozen and keep a stash in the freezer.

serves
2–4

Q

10 oz. spaghetti

½ cup peas (fresh or frozen)

½ cup crème fraîche or sour cream

a handful of mint, freshly chopped

salt and black pepper

Bring a large saucepan of water to a boil and add a pinch of salt. Drop in the pasta and cook according to the instructions on the package. About 2 minutes before the pasta is cooked add the peas to the boiling water.

Drain the pasta and peas and return them to the warm pan with the crème fraîche or sour cream, and mint. Gently toss to combine and coat the pasta in the softened crème fraîche. Season well with salt and pepper and serve.

fusilli with tomatoey sauce

fusilli with *tomatoey* sauce

This sauce is more substantial and has a stronger flavor than basic tomato sauce—it contains celery, carrot, and onion, finely chopped so that they blend in with the tomatoes. Simmer for an hour to allow the sauce time to thicken and become richer.

serves
4–6

2 tablespoons butter

2 tablespoons olive oil, plus extra to serve

1 small celery rib, finely chopped

1 small carrot, finely chopped

1 small onion, finely chopped

a small handful of basil or other herbs, freshly chopped

2 lbs. tomatoes, seeded and chopped

1 lb. dried fusilli

salt and black pepper

grated Parmesan, to serve

Heat the butter and olive oil in a heavy-based saucepan over high heat. When it starts to bubble, add the celery, carrot, onion, herbs, and tomatoes. Stir quickly in the hot fat for a few minutes, then lower the heat, cover, and simmer for 1 hour. Stir from time to time, adding a little water as the tomatoes reduce.

Bring a large saucepan of water to a boil and add a pinch of salt. Drop in the pasta and cook according to the instructions on the package.

Push the sauce though a strainer. Add salt and pepper to taste. Toss the sauce through the warm pasta, then sprinkle with Parmesan.

pasta with *purple sprouting broccoli, chile,* and *pine nuts*

Purple sprouting broccoli is sweeter and more tender than regular broccoli. It's a little dearer but worth it for this dish.

serves
4

14 oz. dried orecchiette, or other small pasta shapes

14 oz. purple sprouting broccoli, chopped

3 tablespoons butter

2 tablespoons olive oil

2 small red chiles, seeded and finely chopped

2 garlic cloves, sliced

¼ cup pine nuts

1 cup grated Parmesan

Bring a large saucepan of water to a boil and add a pinch of salt. Drop in the pasta and cook according to the instructions on the package. Drain and return to the warm pan.

Bring another saucepan of water to a boil and add a pinch of salt. Cook the broccoli florets for 2 minutes and drain well.

Heat the butter and oil in a skillet over medium heat. When it starts to bubble, add the chiles, garlic, and pine nuts and cook for 3–4 minutes, stirring often, until the garlic has softened and the pine nuts are starting to turn golden. Add the broccoli and stir to coat in the other ingredients. Add the broccoli mixture to the pasta with the Parmesan and stir well.

spaghetti with tomatoes and eggplant

serves 4

14 oz. dried spaghetti
or penne

1 eggplant, about 12 oz.,
cubed

1 lb. cherry tomatoes, halved
and seeded

½ cup olive oil

½ cup passata (strained
tomatoes) or tomato juice

2 garlic cloves, chopped

a large handful of basil,
leaves torn, to serve

salt and black pepper

No long simmering needed for this pasta sauce: the tiny tomato halves are oven-roasted and the cubes of eggplant salted, then sautéed, to intensify the tastes. Use whatever sturdy dry pasta is available: spaghetti, penne, and rigatoni all taste excellent in this context. The sauce is relatively dry and relatively minimal. It is deliberate—it works!

Preheat the oven to 450°F.

Bring a large saucepan of salted water to a boil, ready to add the pasta when the vegetables are half cooked.

Put the eggplant cubes in a nonmetal bowl, then add 1 teaspoon salt and set aside while you cook the tomatoes.

Pack the tomatoes, cut sides up, on a baking sheet, sprinkle with salt, and drizzle with 2 tablespoons of the oil. Roast in the preheated oven for 10 minutes or until wilted and aromatic.

Cook the pasta according to the instructions on the package.

Drain the eggplant and pat dry with paper towels. Heat 4 tablespoons of the olive oil in a nonstick skillet. Add the eggplant and cook, stirring, over high heat until frizzled and soft, about 8 minutes. Add the roasted tomato halves, passata or juice, garlic, and black pepper. Cook, stirring, for 2–3 minutes, then stir through most of the basil.

Drain the pasta and return to the saucepan. Toss in the remaining olive oil. Divide between bowls and spoon over the sauce. Garnish with the remaining basil leaves.

rigatoni with roasted vegetables

rigatoni with roasted vegetables

When choosing bell peppers, eggplants, tomatoes, and the like, squeeze them lightly to ensure the flesh is firm. Don't worry if they're funny shapes, it's more important that they are fresh.

serves
4

Preheat the oven to 400°F.

Bring a large saucepan of water to a boil and add a pinch of salt. Drop in the pasta and cook according to the instructions on the package.

Cut the eggplant, bell peppers, zucchini, and leeks into bite-size pieces, about 1 inch square, and arrange in a single layer in a roasting pan. Add the rosemary, garlic, and olive oil and mix well. Cover with aluminum foil and roast in the preheated oven for 20–30 minutes until tender.

Discard the foil, add the capers and tomatoes, stir, and roast for 10 minutes.

Drain the pasta and stir into the roasted vegetables. Serve with Parmesan.

14 oz. dried rigatoni or penne

1 small eggplant, about 4 oz.

1 red bell pepper, seeded

1 yellow bell pepper, seeded

1 medium zucchini

1 leek

1½ tablespoons freshly chopped rosemary leaves

2 garlic cloves, crushed

2 tablespoons olive oil

1–2 tablespoons capers, rinsed and drained

½ cup cherry tomatoes

grated Parmesan, to serve

farfalle with roasted squash, feta, and sage

Roasting the squash and onion first adds a slightly smoky flavor to this pasta sauce. You can use either butternut squash or pumpkin—in either case you will need a 2-lb. vegetable to yield 1¼ lbs. flesh.

serves
4

Preheat the oven to 425°F.

Put the squash, onion, sage, 1 tablespoon of the olive oil, and some seasoning in a roasting pan, toss well, and roast in the preheated oven for 30 minutes, or until the vegetables are golden and cooked through.

Bring a large saucepan of water to a boil and add a pinch of salt. Drop in the pasta and cook according to the instructions on the package.

Heat the remaining oil in a large skillet and gently fry the garlic, pepper flakes, and a little salt and pepper for 2–3 minutes until soft. Add the pine nuts and fry for 2–3 minutes until lightly browned. Add the roasted squash, onions, sage, and the feta. Drain the pasta, add to the skillet and stir.

1¼ lbs. butternut squash or pumpkin flesh, diced

1 small red onion, thinly sliced

1 tablespoon freshly chopped sage

¼ cup olive oil

14 oz. dried farfalle

4 garlic cloves, finely chopped

a pinch of hot red pepper flakes

⅛ cup pine nuts

7 oz. feta, diced

salt and black pepper

big pasta shells stuffed with herbs and ricotta

14 oz. dried conchiglioni rigati

3 tomatoes, seeded and chopped

2 cups ricotta

2 tablespoons freshly chopped herbs, such as chives, parsley, and basil

3 tablespoons olive oil

3 tablespoons grated Parmesan

serves
4

Q

This is ingenious really—a cheat's version of stuffed pasta which requires no time and no skill but still tastes scrumptious.

Preheat the oven to 350°F.

Bring a large saucepan of water to a boil and add a pinch of salt. Drop in the pasta and cook according to the instructions on the package. Drain well.

Put the tomatoes in a bowl and stir in the ricotta and mixed herbs. Place a teaspoonful of the mixture into each of the pasta shells and lay them snugly in a baking dish.

Drizzle over the olive oil and scatter over the Parmesan. Bake in the preheated oven for 10 minutes, until hot.

linguine with ricotta, cinnamon, and walnuts

1 lb. dried linguine or rigatoni

1 cup ricotta

4 tablespoons unsalted butter, softened

1 teaspoon confectioners' sugar

1 teaspoon cinnamon or apple pie spice

½ cup chopped walnuts

salt and black pepper

grated Parmesan, to serve

serves
4–6

Q

This is an ideal vegetarian meal—it is more a dressing than a sauce, because there is no cooking. It's so straightforward, it can be prepared in the time it takes to cook the pasta.

Bring a large saucepan of water to a boil and add a pinch of salt. Drop in the pasta and cook according to the instructions on the package. Drain well, reserving ½ cup of the pasta cooking water.

Put the ricotta, butter, confectioners' sugar, and cinnamon in a bowl and beat with a wooden spoon until smooth and creamy. Add salt and pepper to taste and stir in half the reserved pasta water.

Add the ricotta mixture to the drained pasta, with the remaining pasta water if necessary, then stir in the chopped walnuts. Mix well until coated. Serve with grated Parmesan.

big pasta shells stuffed with herbs and ricotta

pasta with basic *cream, butter,* and *parmesan* sauce

1 cup light cream

2 tablespoons unsalted butter

3 tablespoons grated Parmesan, plus extra to serve

8 oz. dried pasta or fresh, stuffed pasta

3 tablespoons freshly chopped herbs, such as parsley, cilantro, or basil

grated peel of ½ lemon (optional)

lots of black pepper

 serves 2-3

 Q

This sauce provides the base for a variety of other sauces. Stir in some vegetables as a feast for unexpected guests. Add herbs, nuts, or cheese to make a delicious sauce for stuffed pasta.

Put the cream and butter in a saucepan over low heat. Bring to simmering point, shaking the pan from time to time. Simmer for a few minutes or until the sauce starts to thicken. Add the Parmesan and pepper and stir.

Bring a large saucepan of water to a boil and add a pinch of salt. Drop in the pasta and cook according to the instructions on the package. Drain well, reserving ⅓ cup of the pasta cooking water.

Stir the sauce and half of the reserved pasta water into the pasta. Mix until well coated. Add extra pasta water if necessary and stir again. Serve sprinkled with extra Parmesan, chopped herbs, and lemon peel, if using.

chile pasta bake

8 oz. dried fettuccine or tagliatelle

2 zucchini, chopped

2 leeks, chopped

2 garlic cloves, crushed

1–2 red chiles, seeded and finely chopped

1 tablespoon freshly chopped oregano

1 tablespoon freshly chopped parsley

2¼ cups passata (strained tomatoes)

3 tablespoons sour cream

2 tablespoons grated Parmesan

salt and black pepper

serves 3-4

Fettuccine and tagliatelle take very little time to cook, which makes them the perfect ingredient for a quick evening meal.

Preheat the oven to 375°F.

Bring a large saucepan of water to a boil and add a pinch of salt. Drop in the pasta and cook according to the instructions on the package.

Heat a large nonstick saucepan over medium heat, add the zucchini, leeks, and garlic and dry fry for 2–3 minutes. Add the chiles, herbs, passata, and sour cream. Drain the pasta and add to the chile sauce. Season to taste with salt and pepper and stir well. Transfer to an ovenproof dish and sprinkle with the grated Parmesan.

Bake in the preheated oven for 30–35 minutes, until golden brown and bubbling. Serve immediately.

pasta with quick
tomato sauce

pasta with quick *tomato* sauce

This classic tomato sauce is made simply with tomatoes, olive oil, garlic, and the flavoring of your choice.

serves
4–6

Put the tomatoes, oil, and garlic in a heavy-based saucepan. Add your choice of flavoring. Cover and simmer over low heat for 30 minutes, or until thickened. Stir from time to time to stop the sauce sticking to the bottom of the pan. Add a little of the reserved tomato juice whenever necessary to keep the sauce moist.

Bring a large saucepan of water to a boil and add a pinch of salt. Drop in the pasta and cook according to the instructions on the package. Drain well.

Discard the garlic and chile or cinnamon stick. Mash the sauce with a potato masher. Taste and adjust the seasoning with salt and pepper. Pour the sauce over the pasta, sprinkle with the Parmesan, and stir well.

2½ lbs. canned chopped tomatoes, drained (reserve the juice)

⅓ cup olive oil

4 garlic cloves

your choice of: 1 small piece of fresh chile, ½ cinnamon stick, ½ teaspoon dried oregano, or a handful of freshly chopped herbs

1 lb. dried pasta or fresh, stuffed pasta

3 tablespoons grated Parmesan

salt and black pepper

extra-crispy *mac* and *cheese*

The best bit about mac and cheese, as we all know, is the crispy topping, so how fantastic would it be to have crispy bits all the way through. Try it and see!

serves
2–3

4–5 oz. sharp cheddar, coarsely grated

2 tablespoons butter

3 tablespoons all-purpose flour

1¼ cups whole milk

6 oz. rigatoni or penne

½ teaspoon mustard

a few drops of Worcestershire sauce

salt and black pepper

a shallow ovenproof dish, lightly buttered

Preheat the oven to 325°F.

Sprinkle 1½ oz. of the cheddar in an even layer over a baking sheet. Bake in the preheated oven for 8–10 minutes until bubbling and beginning to brown. Remove from the oven, let cool, then break into pieces and set aside.

Put the butter in a medium nonstick saucepan and melt gently. Stir in the flour and cook for a few seconds, then take the pan off the heat and add the milk little by little, stirring before you add the next amount. Put the pan back on the stove, increase the heat slightly, then bring the sauce gradually to a boil, stirring continuously. Turn the heat right down again and let the sauce simmer for 5 minutes, stirring it occasionally.

Bring a large saucepan of water to a boil and add a pinch of salt. Drop in the pasta and cook according to the instructions on the package.

Meanwhile, preheat the broiler.

Just before the pasta is ready, stir half the remaining cheddar into the sauce, add the mustard and Worcestershire sauce, and season to taste. Add a little more milk if it looks too thick.

Drain the pasta thoroughly and tip into the prepared ovenproof dish. Scatter the crispy cheese pieces over the pasta and mix together. Pour in the cheese sauce, then sprinkle over the remaining cheddar. Place the dish under the hot broiler for about 5 minutes until the top is brown and crispy.

mac 'n' greens

3 tablespoons butter

1 medium/large leek, trimmed and thinly sliced

⅓ cup all-purpose flour

2½ cups lowfat milk

a head of broccoli divided into small florets (about 10 oz. florets)

12 oz. dried penne (plain or whole-wheat)

2 handfuls of chard or spinach leaves

5 oz. mature Gruyère

3 heaping tablespoons grated Parmesan

salt, black pepper, and grated nutmeg

4 individual ovenproof dishes, lightly buttered

serves 4

This is a healthy twist on mac and cheese if you feel that you've had too much indulgent food recently. You can also use whole-wheat pasta if you want to make this recipe even more nutritionally balanced.

Put the butter in a medium nonstick saucepan and melt gently. Add the leeks, stir, and cook for 1 minute, then stir in the flour and cook for a few seconds. Take the pan off the heat and gradually add the milk, stirring continuously. Put the pan back on the stove, increase the heat slightly, then bring the milk gradually up to simmering point. Turn the heat right down again and leave the sauce over very low heat.

Fill a large saucepan with boiling water, bring back to a boil, add salt, then add the broccoli and blanch for a couple of minutes. Transfer the broccoli to a strainer with a slotted spoon and rinse with cold water. Tip the pasta into the same water in the pan and cook according to the instructions on the package.

Wash and remove the stalk and central rib from the chard or spinach (unless using baby leaves). Just before the pasta is ready, stir half the Gruyère and the Parmesan into the sauce and check the seasoning, adding salt, pepper, nutmeg, and more Parmesan, if necessary. Add the broccoli and chard or spinach, stir, and set aside for 3–4 minutes.

Meanwhile, preheat the broiler.

Drain the pasta and divide between the prepared dishes. Pour over the sauce and vegetables and mix gently, then sprinkle over the remaining Gruyère. Place the dishes on a baking sheet and broil for 5 minutes until the cheese is brown and bubbling.

light entrées

bean and vegetable soup

bean and *vegetable* soup

This is a little like minestrone and it's packed with vegetables. The vegetables are lightly steamed, not fried, before cooking in the stock, making it a particularly good option when you are on a healthy eating drive. It's delicious with a large chunk of whole-wheat bread.

In a large saucepan, soften the onion and garlic in 4 tablespoons of the stock for 5 minutes, with the lid on. Stir in the carrots, mushrooms, and zucchini, season, and cook for 2 minutes. Stir in the passata and the remaining stock and bring to a simmer, then cover and cook for 10 minutes.

Mix in the beans and cabbage, re-cover the pan, and simmer for a further 10 minutes. Adjust the seasoning and stir in the basil just before serving.

serves 6

1 onion, chopped

2 garlic cloves, crushed

5 cups vegetable stock

2 carrots, diced

2 cups mushrooms, chopped

2 zucchini, diced

3 cups passata (strained tomatoes)

14-oz. can cannellini beans, drained and rinsed

1¼ cups shredded green cabbage

3 tablespoons freshly chopped basil

salt and black pepper

white bean soup with *olive* gremolata

You can make this soup with any canned white beans, such as navy, cannellini, or lima beans. The tasty olive gremolata that you spoon on top makes the soup a bit more special.

Heat the oil in a large saucepan and fry the onion, garlic, and sage for 5 minutes until golden. Add the potatoes and beans, stir well, then add the stock, bay leaf, and some salt and pepper.

Bring to a boil, cover, and simmer gently for 20 minutes until the potatoes are tender. If you like, you can transfer half the soup to a blender or food processor, or use a handheld blender, and blend until smooth, or you can mash half of it with a potato masher. Return to the pan, adjust the seasoning, and heat through.

Meanwhile, to make the olive gremolata, finely chop the olives and mix with lemon peel and parsley. Serve the soup in bowls topped with the gremolata.

serves 6

¼ cup olive oil

1 large onion, chopped

2 garlic cloves, crushed

1 teaspoon dried sage

1 lb. baking potatoes, cubed

2 x 14-oz. cans white beans, such as navy, cannellini, or lima, rinsed and drained

4 cups vegetable stock

1 dried bay leaf

salt and black pepper

Olive gremolata

1 cup pitted black olives

grated peel of 1 lemon

2 tablespoons freshly chopped parsley

roasted *vegetable* soup

Once everything is peeled and chopped, this rustic chunky soup is surprisingly simple to make. The vegetables are roasted in the oven, which makes their flavor sweet but intense.

1½ lbs. ripe plum tomatoes, halved

1 red onion, finely chopped

2 carrots, finely chopped

1 small red chile

2 garlic cloves, peeled but left whole

a few thyme or rosemary sprigs

2 tablespoons olive oil

1⅓ cups passata (strained tomatoes)

½ teaspoon sugar

a squeeze of lime juice

salt and black pepper

a handful of cilantro, freshly chopped

Preheat the oven to 400°F.

Put the tomatoes, onion, and carrots in a roasting pan. Add the chile, garlic, thyme or rosemary sprigs, and olive oil and toss until the vegetables are well coated. Roast in the preheated oven for about 25 minutes, turning the vegetables occasionally using a large spoon.

Remove from the oven and discard the chile. Blend the roasted vegetables, garlic, and herbs with the passata in a blender or food processor, or using a handheld blender. Add the sugar, lime juice, and ⅔ cup water, and season well with salt and pepper.

Pour the mixture into a large saucepan and gently heat through. Add the chopped cilantro just before serving.

creamy *pea* soup

This is creamy and dreamy and you can make it with frozen peas, so it's quick as well as delicious!

3 tablespoons olive oil

1 small onion, chopped

1 garlic clove, crushed

1 small potato, about 3 oz., chopped

1½ lbs. peas (fresh or frozen)

4 cups vegetable stock

3 tablespoons heavy cream

salt and black pepper

Heat the olive oil in a large saucepan, then add the onion, garlic, and potato. Cook over gentle heat for about 8–10 minutes, stirring quite often, until the onion is shiny and the potatoes are starting to soften.

Pour in the peas and the stock. Leave the soup to simmer for about 20 minutes, until the potato is very soft—the potatoes should be easily squashed when you press them with a wooden spoon.

Blend the soup in a blender or food processor, or using a handheld blender. Stir in the cream and season to taste with a little salt and pepper.

roasted vegetable soup

tomato and red lentil soup

serves
4

This tomato soup is thickened with split red lentils and is packed with delicious ingredients. Adding a couple of tablespoons of cream at the end makes it that little bit more luxurious—you can use any cream you like.

1 tablespoon olive oil

1 red onion, finely chopped

1 carrot, finely chopped

1 celery rib, finely chopped

1 garlic clove, crushed

14-oz. can chopped tomatoes

1 tablespoon tomato paste

¼ cup split red lentils

1¾ cups vegetable stock

a big pinch of salt

a big pinch of black pepper

a big pinch of sugar

2 tablespoons cream, to serve

Heat the oil in a large saucepan over low heat. Put the onion, carrot, celery, and garlic into the pan. Stir gently with a wooden spoon, then cover the pan with a lid and let cook very slowly for 5 minutes. Add the tomatoes, tomato paste, red lentils, stock, salt, pepper, and sugar. Stir well, then turn up the heat so the mixture comes to a boil.

When the soup has boiled, cover the pan with the lid, then turn down the heat. Simmer for 30 minutes, stirring occasionally.

At the end of the cooking time, take off the lid, turn off the heat, and let the soup cool for 5 minutes.

Blend the soup in a blender or food processor, or using a handheld blender. Taste—add more salt, pepper, or sugar as needed—then carefully warm up the soup over low heat. Stir in the cream and serve.

poached *mushrooms* with *egg noodles*

serves
4

The purity and natural flavors of this noodle dish will make you feel very healthy! Try using tofu instead of mushrooms.

4 portobello mushrooms

1 leek, trimmed and chopped

4 shallots

1 dried bay leaf

8 oz. dried egg noodles

2 zucchini, chopped

4 oz. baby sweet corn, trimmed

4 oz. flat beans, sliced

4 oz. spinach, chopped

1 tablespoon soy sauce

salt and black pepper

Put the mushrooms into a large saucepan and add the leeks, shallots, bay leaf, salt, and pepper. Add water to cover and heat until simmering. Cover with a lid and cook for 20 minutes.

Add the noodles, adding extra water to cover if necessary. Add the zucchini, sweet corn, beans, spinach, and soy sauce. Simmer for a further 4 minutes, until the noodles and all the vegetables are cooked. Serve in bowls with a ladle of the cooking juices.

tomato and red lentil soup

french onion soup

french *onion* soup

This is a popular favorite with lots of people, and is filling enough to be a meal in itself.

serves
4–6

Put the butter and oil in a large saucepan and heat until the butter melts. Add the onions and salt and stir well. Cook over low heat for 20–30 minutes or until the onions are golden brown. Sprinkle the flour over the onions and stir for 2–3 minutes until there is no sign of white specks of flour. Pour a ladle of the stock onto the onions. Stir well, add the remaining stock and simmer, part-covered, for another 20–30 minutes. Add salt and pepper to taste.

Meanwhile, preheat the oven to 325°F.

To make the croutons, put the bread on a baking sheet and toast in the preheated oven for 15 minutes. Brush with the olive oil and rub with the cut garlic clove. Return to the oven for 15 minutes or until the bread is quite dry.

Ladle the soup into heatproof bowls. Put the slices of toast on top and pile the cheese over them. Dot with more butter and cook in the hot oven for about 15 minutes until the cheese has melted.

3 tablespoons unsalted butter, plus extra to finish

1 tablespoon olive oil

2 lbs. onions, thinly sliced

1 teaspoon salt

⅓ cup flour

4 cups hot vegetable stock

salt and black pepper

Croutons

8–12 thick slices of bread (about 1 inch thick)

1 tablespoon olive oil

1 large garlic clove, halved

1 cup grated Gruyère

indian omelet

indian omelet

Serve this hot or cold, cut into wedges, with chutney or a raita on the side. Choose a raita of your choice from page 20.

serves
2–3

Q

Break the eggs into a bowl, add the yogurt, and whisk briefly with a fork, just enough to mix the yolks and whites. Stir in the cumin, cilantro, garlic, and some salt and pepper.

Heat 1 tablespoon of the oil in a small skillet. Add the onion, chile, and ginger and fry over medium-high heat for 2–3 minutes, then add the tomatoes and cook for 1–2 minutes. Using a slotted spoon, transfer to the egg mixture and stir gently.

Add the remaining oil to the skillet and swirl it around to coat the bottom and sides. Pour the egg mixture into the skillet, reduce the heat to low, and cook for about 5–6 minutes, or until the top is almost set.

Slide under a preheated broiler to finish cooking or put a plate over the top of the skillet and invert so the omelet falls onto the plate. Slide back into the skillet and cook for 1–2 minutes. Cut into wedges and serve with raita.

4 large eggs

2 tablespoons plain yogurt

1 teaspoon ground cumin

2 tablespoons freshly chopped cilantro

1 garlic clove, crushed

2 tablespoons safflower oil

1 onion, finely chopped

1 small red chile, seeded and chopped

1 inch fresh ginger, peeled and grated

2 tomatoes, finely chopped

salt and black pepper

omelet with *chives* and *cheese*

A perfectly crumpled, soft omelet oozing with cheese is bliss—perfect for one, when you need something fast and delicious.

serves
1

Q

Break the eggs into a bowl, add half the chives and some salt and pepper, and whisk briefly with a fork.

Heat a small skillet over high heat until really hot. Add the butter, wait for it to sizzle, then pour in the eggs. Let them become nicely golden on the outside—no more than 45 seconds—drawing the cooked edges into the center. Tilt the skillet so the uncooked egg runs into the edges. When the omelet is evenly set, except for a little unset egg, it is done.

Remove the skillet from the heat and add the Gruyère or cheddar and cream in the center of the omelet. Fold 2 edges of the omelet over, then tilt the skillet so you can slide it out and upturn it onto a plate, folded side down. Sprinkle some pepper over the top and finish with the remaining chives.

3 eggs

2 tablespoons snipped chives

1 tablespoon butter

2 tablespoons grated Gruyère or cheddar

1 tablespoon heavy cream

salt and black pepper

cauliflower and caperberries on halloumi

If you don't fancy halloumi but like the sound of the flavors in this recipe, the cauliflower mixture could also be served as a topping on thick toast.

3 tablespoons olive oil

5 oz. cauliflower, broken into small florets

1 garlic clove, chopped

a handful of caperberries, large ones halved, or capers, drained and rinsed

⅓ cup pitted green olives, sliced

1 tablespoon freshly chopped parsley

2 teaspoons lemon juice

5 oz. halloumi, cut into ¼-inch-thick slices

salt and black pepper

Heat 2 tablespoons of the olive oil in a skillet and cook the cauliflower for 8–10 minutes over high heat, stirring often until it browns evenly and starts to crisp up. Add the garlic, caperberries, olives, parsley, and lemon juice and cook for 2 minutes, stirring constantly. Season to taste and leave in the skillet to keep warm.

Heat the remaining olive oil in a nonstick skillet over high heat. Cook the halloumi slices for 1 minute on each side, until golden brown. Transfer the halloumi to plates and spoon the warm cauliflower mixture over each one.

tofu and vegetable wraps

You will need to marinate the tofu for these wraps for an hour so that they soak up all the sweet, spicy flavors.

6 oz. firm tofu

2 large soft tortillas

1 carrot, grated

½ red bell pepper, seeded and cut into thin strips

a handful of arugula

salt and black pepper

olive oil, for brushing

Marinade

2 tablespoons soy sauce

1 tablespoon honey

1 tablespoon sweet chili sauce

2 tablespoons tomato ketchup

Pat the tofu dry with a paper towel and cut it into 4 thick strips. Mix together the ingredients for the marinade in a shallow dish. Add the tofu and spoon the marinade over until well covered. Cover and marinate for 1 hour.

Lightly brush a ridged grill pan or skillet with olive oil and heat until hot. Arrange the tofu in the skillet and grill for 3 minutes each side until golden and it bears the marks of the grill pan.

Warm the tortillas—either wrap in foil and warm in the oven or warm in a dry skillet. Put 2 pieces of tofu down the center of each tortilla and spoon over any remaining marinade. Divide the carrot, bell pepper, and arugula between the tortillas, season to taste, then fold in the ends and sides of each tortilla to make a package. Cut in half horizontally before serving.

cauliflower and caperberries
on *halloumi*

baked *mushrooms*

Baked mushrooms often come swimming in oil in order to bring out their flavor. This can leave you feeling overloaded before you even get to the end of the meal! This recipe, however, uses garlic, chiles, and chives to give lots of flavor, so the fat content can remain low.

serves
4

8 oz. cremini or portobello mushrooms, wiped

2–4 teaspoons olive oil

1 celery rib, finely chopped

1–2 large garlic cloves, crushed

1 green chile, seeded and finely chopped

½ cup bread crumbs (preferably fresh)

1 tomato, seeded and chopped

2 tablespoons snipped chives

salt and black pepper

Preheat the oven to 350°F.

Choose 4 portobello or 8 cremini mushrooms and remove the stalks. Put the caps stem-side up in an ovenproof dish. Finely chop the remaining mushrooms and all the stalks.

Heat a nonstick skillet and add 2 teaspoons of the oil. Add the chopped mushrooms, celery, garlic, and chile and fry, stirring frequently, until soft. Let cool slightly, then transfer to a bowl.

Add the bread crumbs, tomato, and chives to the bowl, then season to taste with salt and pepper. Mix well, adding a little oil to moisten, if necessary. Fill the mushrooms with the bread-crumb mixture. Pour about 4 tablespoons water into the dish, then cook in the preheated oven for 12–15 minutes, until the mushrooms are soft and the topping is crisp. Remove from the oven and serve immediately.

Variation For a really quick version (and if you have a blender or food processor), prepare the mushrooms as above. Put the remaining mushrooms with 2 garlic cloves, 2 oz. whole-wheat bread, 6 scallions, 2 oz. dried apricots, 2 tablespoons pecans, and 2 tablespoons cilantro leaves in the blender or food processor. Add salt and pepper, to taste. Blend, adding a little lemon juice if necessary, to give a moist stuffing. Fill the mushrooms with this mixture and cook as above.

cottage cheese pancakes with *sweet chili mushrooms*

1¼ cups self-rising flour

2 large eggs

¾ cup milk

½ cup cottage cheese

a large pinch of salt

safflower oil, for frying

Sweet chili mushrooms

2 large flat mushrooms, sliced

2–3 tablespoons sweet chili sauce

serves 2

The batter here makes about 15 pancakes—obviously too many for two people, but the remainder can be chilled or frozen for future use. This is the kind of versatile dish that you can enjoy at any time of day—it's especially good for a hearty breakfast.

Put the flour, eggs, milk, cottage cheese, and salt in a blender or food processor and blend to a smooth batter. Set the batter aside for 30 minutes to rest.

Lightly oil a large nonstick skillet and pour a ladle of the batter into the skillet to form a round pancake—you will probably be able to cook about 3 pancakes at a time. Cook the pancakes for 1½–2 minutes per side until golden. Keep the pancakes you've already made warm while you make the rest.

When all the batter is used, wipe the skillet clean, then add 1 tablespoon oil. Fry the mushrooms for about 5 minutes until tender, then remove from the heat and stir in the sweet chili sauce and 1 tablespoon water.

To serve, put 3 pancakes on each plate and top with the mushrooms. Spoon over any sauce left in the skillet.

Variation To make cottage cheese and corn pancakes, stir ¾ cup canned, drained corn kernels into the batter mixture after it has rested. The corn pancakes are delicious with sliced avocado, or if you're feeding meat-eaters, with bacon and a drizzle of maple syrup.

*raw tomato and herb sauce
on grilled polenta*

raw *tomato* and *herb* sauce on grilled *polenta*

This raw sauce is so versatile. Spoon it onto this great polenta base, or use it as a chunky topping for many dishes, like pasta.

Cook the polenta according to the instructions on the package, adding a little salt and pepper to the mixture. Pour onto the baking sheet and form into a mound. Alternatively, pour into the cake pan. Let set for at least 1 hour, then cut into 4 slices. If the cooled polenta is too thick, slice it in half horizontally, then cut into slices.

To make the raw tomato and herb sauce, put the tomatoes, scallions, herbs, salt, and pepper into a bowl. Pour over the olive oil and stir gently. Set aside for about 30 minutes so the flavors mingle.

Heat a grill pan or skillet until very hot. Working in batches, brush the polenta pieces with olive oil and cook for a few minutes on each side until golden and barred with grill marks. Remove from the pan and keep warm in a low oven while you cook the rest. Put the polenta onto plates and spoon the sauce over the top to serve.

1 cup instant polenta

Raw tomato and herb sauce

1 lb. ripe tomatoes, seeded and finely chopped

2 scallions, finely chopped

1 tablespoon freshly chopped parsley

1 tablespoon freshly chopped thyme

¼ cup olive oil, plus extra for brushing

salt and black pepper

a baking sheet or round cake pan, 8 inches in diameter, oiled

asparagus with *parmesan* and chopped *eggs*

Asparagus and Parmesan are pricey, so this is best kept for a special treat. Try to shave the Parmesan with a vegetable peeler because you'll getter bigger, nicer chunks than if you grate it.

Hard-boil the eggs following the instructions in the Avocado and Chickpea Salad recipe on page 45. Drain, cool, shell, chop, and set aside.

Meanwhile, trim the asparagus: snap or cut off any woody ends from the stems. Put in a covered saucepan with a small amount of water and steam for about 10 minutes, or until tender and still bright green, depending on the thickness. The tip of a sharp knife should glide easily into the thickest part of the stem when cooked. Drain well and toss with olive oil, salt, and pepper, then sprinkle the chopped eggs and Parmesan shavings over the top.

4 eggs

1 lb. asparagus

¼ cup olive oil

3 oz. Parmesan, shaved with a vegetable peeler

salt and black pepper

hearty entrées

stir-fried *tofu* with crisp *greens* and *mushrooms*

This stir-fry is very fresh and very Thai in its simplicity and balance of flavors. You will only need to quickly cook the greens in boiling water to soften them a little, which will also bring out their brilliant emerald green color. The mushrooms, available from any specialty Asian store, are a fantastic pantry staple—they are inexpensive and will keep indefinitely in an airtight container. The trick with drying out the tofu on paper towels is one you can use for other recipes using soft tofu and is especially good for fried tofu dishes.

Put the tofu on several sheets of paper towel and leave for 20–30 minutes to absorb excess moisture. Put the mushrooms in a heatproof bowl and cover with boiling water. Set aside for 20 minutes. Drain the mushrooms, remove the stems, and halve any larger ones.

Blanch the vegetables in boiling water for 30 seconds, until bright emerald green and softened. Drain and cover with cold water to stop them cooking further. When cold, drain well.

Heat a wok over high heat, then add the oil. Cook the tofu cubes in the hot oil for 5 minutes, turning often, until light golden and puffed. Transfer the tofu to paper towels and pour off all but 2 tablespoons of oil from the wok.

Add the vegetables to the wok and stir-fry for 2 minutes. Add the mushrooms and gently stir-fry for 1 minute. Add the garlic and stir-fry for 1 minute, then add the soy sauce, pepper, sugar, and 2 tablespoons water to the wok. Return the tofu to the wok and stir-fry gently for 1 minute to coat all the ingredients in the sauce, being careful not to break up the tofu. Remove the wok from the heat and serve with steamed jasmine rice, if you like.

serves
4

10 oz. soft tofu, cut into 1-inch cubes

8 dried Chinese mushrooms

2 oz. sugar snap peas, trimmed

2 oz. snow peas, trimmed

2 bunches of fine asparagus, cut into 2-inch lengths

¼ cup vegetable oil

2 garlic cloves, crushed

1 tablespoon light soy sauce

a pinch of white or black pepper

a pinch of sugar

stir-fried *vegetables* with *five-spice tofu*

½ teaspoon Chinese
five-spice powder

8 oz. firm tofu, cut into
1-inch cubes

2 tablespoons vegetable oil

3 garlic cloves, crushed

7 oz. small broccoli florets

7 oz. bok choy, sliced

7 oz. snow peas

1 large carrot, cut into
matchsticks

1 red bell pepper, seeded and
cut into matchsticks

3 oz. canned water chestnuts,
drained and sliced

3 oz. canned sliced bamboo
shoots, drained and rinsed

Sauce

2 tablespoons vegetarian
"oyster" sauce

2 tablespoons light soy sauce

½ cup vegetable stock

1 tablespoon cornstarch,
combined with 2 tablespoons
cold water

serves
4

Q

This is a hearty and flavorful vegetarian dish, called Buddha's delight, traditionally eaten on the first day of Chinese New Year —Buddhists believe that meat should not be eaten on the first five days of the year. Every Buddhist family has their own version and ingredients vary from cook to cook.

Combine all the sauce ingredients in a bowl and set aside.

Sprinkle the five-spice powder over the tofu.

Heat the oil in a wok or large skillet until hot. Add the tofu in batches and stir-fry over high heat until golden all over. Remove the tofu from the wok and drain well on paper towels.

Add the garlic to the hot wok and stir-fry for 1 minute, or until golden. Add the broccoli, bok choy, snow peas, carrot, and bell pepper with a sprinkle of water and stir-fry over high heat for 2–3 minutes. Finally, throw in the water chestnuts and bamboo shoots.

Pour the sauce into the wok and bring to a boil, then reduce the heat and simmer gently for 2 minutes, or until the sauce has thickened. Divide between 4 bowls and serve with rice or noodles.

1 tablespoon sesame oil

1 onion, sliced

8 oz. green beans, halved

12 oz. deep-fried tofu, sliced

2 tablespoons sweet
chili sauce

a handful of basil leaves

2 tablespoons sesame seeds,
toasted in a dry skillet

Chili coconut sauce

1 lemon grass stalk

1¾ cups coconut milk

1½ cups vegetable stock

1 tablespoon Thai fish sauce
(see Introduction, right)

8 lime leaves, sliced

2 garlic cloves, chopped

1 inch fresh ginger, peeled
and grated

¼ cup safflower oil

4 eggs, lightly beaten

6 oz. dried thick rice noodles,
soaked in warm water for
5 minutes, then drained

4 oz. kale or other leafy green,
tough central core removed
and leaves chopped

2 tablespoons lime juice

¼ cup sweet chili sauce

¼ cup light soy sauce

1 large carrot, grated

1 cup bean sprouts

To serve

⅓ cup roasted peanuts,
chopped

4 scallions, finely sliced

a handful of cilantro

serves **4**

stir-fried *tofu* with *chili coconut* sauce

Deep-fried tofu is available from Asian stores or health food stores where they can be found in the refrigerator. You can substitute ordinary firm tofu, cut into cubes instead. If you are strictly vegetarian and will not eat fish sauce, you can buy a vegetarian "fish" sauce which is made from soy beans. If you can't find it, use light soy sauce as a substitute.

To make the chili coconut sauce, snap the lemon grass stalk in half. Put it, with all the other sauce ingredients, in a saucepan. Bring to a boil and simmer for 20 minutes until reduced by half. Strain the sauce and reserve.

Heat the oil in a wok or skillet and stir-fry the onions and beans for 1 minute, add the tofu, and stir-fry for a further 1 minute. Add the coconut sauce, sweet chili sauce, and basil leaves and heat through. Serve sprinkled with the sesame seeds.

pad thai *noodles*

serves **4**

Pad Thai is probably the best-known of all Thai noodle dishes and it takes only 5 minutes to cook. Use thick ribbonlike rice noodles ("rice sticks") for authenticity, or rice vermicelli or egg noodles. The best thing about this dish is that you can use almost anything as the base for it, so if you are feeding meat-eating friends, you can add some chopped, cooked chicken or even shrimp to their portion.

Heat a wok until very hot, then add the oil. Add the eggs and noodles and stir-fry for about 2 minutes, until the eggs are lightly scrambled. Add the remaining ingredients and stir-fry for a further 3–5 minutes, until the noodles are cooked. Divide between 4 warmed bowls and serve sprinkled with the peanuts, scallions, and cilantro.

*stir-fried
mushrooms*

*stir-fried tofu with
chili coconut sauce*

stir-fried *mushrooms*

Try to use an assortment of mushrooms in this recipe. They are cooked here with the famous "Chinese Trinity" of stir-fry tastes —aromatic garlic, ginger, and scallions.

serves
4

Q

Clean the mushrooms with a soft cloth and trim the stems if necessary. Chop the larger mushrooms in half.

Heat the oil in a wok. Add the garlic, ginger, and scallions and stir-fry for about 20 seconds, then add the firmer kinds of mushrooms. Stir-fry for a few minutes, add the sugar and soy sauce, and stir-fry quickly until the sugar is dissolved. Add the softer mushrooms, turning gently in the sauce without breaking them up. Transfer to a serving plate and serve with rice or noodles.

2 lbs. assorted mushrooms

2 tablespoons vegetable oil

2 garlic cloves, crushed

1 inch fresh ginger, peeled and grated

6 scallions, finely sliced

1 teaspoon sugar

2 teaspoons dark soy sauce

egg noodles stir-fried with vegetables and red curry paste

serves 4

Q

This quick stir-fry mélange is widely popular because it offers something to suit almost any taste. The curry paste provides the hot flavor and the vegetables add a wholesome crispness. Be aware that some brands of red curry paste contain traces of seafood. However, there are many vegetarian-friendly brands so just check the ingredients carefully before you choose one.

8 oz. egg noodles

2 tablespoons safflower oil

2 garlic cloves, chopped

1 tablespoon red curry paste (see Introduction, right)

3 oz. oyster mushrooms, sliced

2 small celery ribs, finely chopped

5 oz. baby sweet corn, halved lengthwise

1 cup bean sprouts

3 scallions, thinly sliced

2 tomatoes, cut into wedges

3 tablespoons light soy sauce

1 teaspoon sugar

Cook the noodles according to the instructions on the package. Drain well.

Heat the oil in a wok. Add the garlic, fry for about 1 minute, then add the curry paste and continue stir-frying until the garlic is golden. Add the noodles, stir well, then add the remaining ingredients. Stir-fry for a couple of minutes.

quick mexican mole

serves 4

Although it may sound unusual, chocolate is the secret ingredient of this Mexican-inspired dish. It adds a wonderfully rich, intense flavor to the vegetables. Serve with boiled rice or a chunk of crusty bread.

2 tablespoons safflower oil

1 red onion, chopped

1 large red bell pepper, seeded and chopped

2 garlic cloves

2 teaspoons ground coriander

1 teaspoon ground cumin

½ teaspoon ground cinnamon

1 lb. sweet potatoes, cubed

14-oz. can chopped tomatoes

14-oz. can red kidney beans, rinsed and drained

2 teaspoons sweet chili sauce

1 oz. dark chocolate, grated

salt and black pepper

Heat the oil in a saucepan and fry the onion, bell pepper, garlic, and spices for 5 minutes. Add the sweet potatoes, tomatoes, beans, chili sauce, and 1¼ cups water and bring to a boil. Cover and simmer gently for 30 minutes.

Stir in the chocolate and cook for a final 5 minutes. Taste and adjust the seasoning with salt and pepper, then serve.

egg noodles stir-fried with vegetables and red curry paste

spinach and *cheese* curry

This is a fabulous vegetarian-friendly curry made with paneer, a firm, fresh white Indian cheese. It's not that easy to find but as luck would have it, halloumi, a cheese from Cyprus, works just as well. The other ingredients are all readily available. Try to have a jar of storebought curry paste on standby in the fridge—it keeps well and saves you from having a cupboard full of dry spices which have a short shelf life. Serve with cooked basmati rice.

serves
4

Q

1 tablespoon vegetable oil

8 oz. paneer or halloumi, cut into 1-inch cubes

2 tablespoons butter

2 tablespoons mild Indian curry paste (Madras or balti)

2 large green chiles (optional), seeded and chopped

1 lb. spinach, roughly chopped

a handful of cilantro, leaves and stems freshly chopped

½ cup light cream

lemon wedges, to serve

Heat the oil in a nonstick skillet over high heat and cook the cubes of cheese for 2–3 minutes, turning often, until golden all over. Remove the cheese to a plate and set aside until needed.

Add the butter to the skillet and when sizzling hot, add the curry paste and green chiles and stir-fry for 2 minutes. Add the spinach and cilantro and cook for 1–2 minutes, until all the spinach has wilted, then stir in the cream.

Add the cheese and cook over low heat for 2–3 minutes, to warm the cheese through. Serve the curry with lemon wedges to squeeze over the top and cooked basmati rice.

quick *vegetable* curry

3 tablespoons safflower oil

1 onion, sliced

2 garlic cloves, chopped

1 inch fresh ginger, peeled and grated

1 tablespoon hot curry paste

1 teaspoon ground cinnamon

1 lb. potatoes, cubed

14-oz. can chopped tomatoes

1¼ cups vegetable stock

1 tablespoon tomato paste

8 oz. button mushrooms, halved

8 oz. peas (fresh or frozen)

⅛ cup ground almonds

2 tablespoons freshly chopped cilantro

salt and black pepper

 serves 4

If you're into fast cooking, this is the ultimate cheat's curry, made with ready-made curry paste. Serve with basmati rice and warm naan bread, if you like. It might strike you as odd to use ground almonds in a curry but in fact it makes the sauce lovely and creamy, without the heaviness of cream itself. Why don't you use your leftover ground almonds for one of the desserts in the last chapter of this book?

Heat the oil in a large saucepan and fry the onion, garlic, ginger, curry paste, and cinnamon for 5 minutes. Add the potatoes, tomatoes, stock, tomato paste, salt, and pepper. Bring to a boil, cover and simmer gently for 20 minutes.

Add the mushrooms, peas, ground almonds, and cilantro to the pan and cook for a further 10 minutes. Taste and adjust the seasoning with salt and pepper, then serve with basmati rice.

cauliflower masala

1 tablespoon safflower oil

2 teaspoons cumin seeds

1 lb. cauliflower florets

2 garlic cloves, thinly sliced

1 inch fresh ginger, peeled and finely chopped

1 green chile, thinly sliced

1 teaspoon garam masala

⅔ cup hot water

juice of ½ lemon

salt and black pepper

 serves 4

In this Indian-inspired recipe, cauliflower florets are stir-fried in a seasoned, spiced oil until just tender. Substitute broccoli florets if you like, to ring the changes.

Heat the safflower oil in a large skillet over medium heat. Add the cumin seeds. Stir-fry for 30 seconds, then add the cauliflower, garlic, ginger, and chile. Turn the heat to high and stir-fry for 6–8 minutes, or until the cauliflower is lightly browned at the edges.

Stir in the garam masala and hot water and stir well. Cover and cook over high heat for 1–2 minutes.

Season well and drizzle with the lemon juice just before serving.

quick vegetable curry

fresh *tomato, pea,* and *paneer* curry

This is such a great, fresh-tasting curry to cook for a small group. It's a real get-stuck-in kind of meal, best enjoyed with lots of accompaniments on the side, like basmati rice, warm naan bread, mango chutney, and maybe even a raita from page 20. As with the Spinach and Cheese Curry on page 115, if you can't find paneer, halloumi is a perfectly good replacement.

serves 4

2 tablespoons vegetable oil

8 oz. paneer, cubed

1 tablespoon butter

2 onions, finely chopped

2 inches fresh ginger, peeled and grated

2 green chiles, seeded and finely chopped

3 ripe tomatoes, chopped

2 teaspoons white wine vinegar

1½ cups frozen peas

½ teaspoon garam masala

a handful of cilantro leaves

salt and black pepper

Heat the oil in a skillet over medium heat. Add the paneer and cook for 4–5 minutes, turning often, until golden all over. Remove from the pan and set aside.

Add the butter to the skillet. When it is melted and sizzling, add the onions and stir-fry until softened and lightly golden. Add the ginger and chiles to the skillet and cook for 1 minute. Add the tomatoes, vinegar, and ¼ cup water and bring to a boil. Cook for about 5 minutes, to thicken slightly. Add the peas and return the paneer to the skillet. Reduce the heat and simmer for about 5 minutes, until the peas are tender.

Stir in the garam masala and season to taste with salt and pepper. Sprinkle with the cilantro leaves and serve with basmati rice and an assortment of Indian accompaniments.

mustardy mushroom stroganoff

serves
1

Q

For nights when you want dinner in a hurry, this can be on the table in just 10 minutes. Serve with basmati and wild rice (which is really good for you!) or couscous, together with some green beans or cabbage.

⅔ cup vegetable stock

½ small onion, sliced

5 oz. mixed mushrooms, chopped if large

1 garlic clove, crushed

1 teaspoon (preferably) grainy mustard

½ teaspoon tomato paste

1 tablespoon sour cream

salt and black pepper

freshly chopped parsley, to serve (optional)

Put 3 tablespoons of the stock in a saucepan. Add the onion, cover the pan, and cook for about 4 minutes or until the onion has softened and the liquid has evaporated.

Stir in the mushrooms, garlic, and some salt and pepper, then add the remaining stock, mustard, and tomato paste. Cook, covered, for 2 minutes, then remove the lid and cook rapidly for 2 minutes to reduce the liquid to a syrup. Stir in the sour cream and parsley, if using, and serve immediately with rice or couscous.

red kidney bean curry

serves
4

Q

A lightly spiced bean curry, this is yummy comfort food, and ready in a matter of minutes. Serve with cooked basmati rice.

1 tablespoon butter

2 tablespoons safflower oil

1 onion, finely chopped

½ teaspoon ground cinnamon

2 dried bay leaves

3 garlic cloves, crushed

1 inch fresh ginger, peeled and finely chopped

½ teaspoon ground turmeric

1 teaspoon ground coriander

2 teaspoons ground cumin

1 teaspoon garam masala

2 dried red chiles

14-oz. can red kidney beans

4 tablespoons tomato paste

salt and black pepper

Heat the butter and safflower oil in a large, heavy-based saucepan and add the onion, cinnamon, bay leaves, garlic, and ginger. Stir-fry for 4–5 minutes. Stir in the turmeric, ground coriander, cumin, garam masala, and chiles.

Add the beans, tomato paste, and a little water to make a thick sauce. Bring to a boil and cook for 4–5 minutes, stirring often. Season well and serve.

mustardy mushroom
stroganoff

ratatouille

ratatouille

Ratatouille is a celebration of summer. It's best made when zucchini, eggplant, and tomatoes are in season so that you get the best flavor. Serve it warm with rice or couscous—it's so good it's guaranteed to please even non-vegetarians.

serves 6

3 tablespoons olive oil

1 onion, sliced

3 garlic cloves, crushed

a small handful of parsley, freshly chopped

1 large eggplant, chopped

2–3 red and/or yellow bell peppers, seeded and chopped

4 zucchini, sliced

¼ teaspoon salt

14-oz. can chopped tomatoes

2 teaspoons red wine vinegar or balsamic vinegar (optional)

salt and black pepper

Heat the oil in a large, heavy-based saucepan over medium heat. Add the onion, garlic, and parsley and sauté for 10 minutes, stirring regularly.

Add the eggplant and cook for 5 minutes. Add the bell peppers and zucchini and stir in the salt. Cook for a few minutes, then add the chopped tomatoes.

Cover and cook for 5 minutes until the tomatoes start to break down, then uncover and cook for 10–15 minutes until the vegetables are tender, adding a little water if necessary. Season to taste with vinegar, if using, and salt and pepper. Serve warm.

lemon and spinach puy lentils with hard-boiled eggs

Puy lentils have a slightly firm texture and nutty flavor, and retain their shape when cooked, unlike other lentils.

serves 2–3

2–3 large eggs

¾ cup Puy or green lentils, rinsed

1 dried bay leaf

1 tablespoon olive oil

1 large onion, chopped

5 tomatoes, seeded and cut into chunks

5 oz. spinach, chopped

2 teaspoons mustard

2 tablespoons crème fraîche or sour cream

juice of 1 lemon

salt and black pepper

Hard-boil the eggs following the instructions in the Avocado and Chickpea Salad recipe on page 45. Drain, cool, shell, halve, and set aside.

Put the lentils and bay leaf in a saucepan. Cover with cold water and bring to a boil. Reduce the heat, half-cover the pan, and cook for 25–30 minutes until tender but not mushy. Drain the lentils and set aside.

Meanwhile, heat the oil in a skillet and fry the onion, covered, for 10 minutes until softened. Add the tomatoes and spinach to the skillet and cook, stirring, for another 2 minutes until the spinach has wilted.

Add the cooked lentils to the skillet with the mustard, crème fraîche, and lemon juice, stirring until everything is combined. Season to taste and warm through. Spoon the lentils onto plates and top with the hard-boiled eggs.

spiced *eggplant* couscous

serves
4

¼ cup vegetable oil

1 large eggplant, cubed

1 tablespoon olive oil

1½ cups couscous

½ teaspoon paprika

½ teaspoon chili powder

1½ cups vegetable stock

a small handful of cilantro, leaves and stems freshly chopped

2 oz. baby spinach

½ cup plain yogurt

lemon wedges, to serve

Popping its head up in just about every style of cuisine, eggplant is very versatile—see the Ratatouille on the previous page, or the Baked Eggplant with Garlic and Tomatoes on page 127. It is just as much at home steamed with scallions and fresh ginger as it is with tomato, basil, and cheese or, as in this dish, with Moroccan spices. You will need one large eggplant, so look for one that is firm, full, and heavy with shiny deep-purple skin. The couscous recipe alone is a treat and can be made on its own for any other occasion.

Heat the vegetable oil in a skillet over high heat and cook the eggplant for 3–4 minutes, turning often so it is an even, golden brown all over. Place on paper towels to drain off the excess oil.

Heat the olive oil in a saucepan over medium heat. Add the couscous, paprika, and chili powder and cook for 2 minutes, stirring constantly. Add the stock and bring to a boil. Remove the pan from the heat, cover with a tight-fitting lid, and let stand for 10 minutes.

Fluff the couscous with a fork, then cover and leave for a further 5 minutes. Place the couscous in a large bowl and add the eggplant, cilantro, and baby spinach and toss to combine.

Place on a plate with the yogurt and lemon wedges on the side to serve.

Variation Replace the eggplant with sliced zucchini. Pan-fry them in a little olive oil until golden on both sides. Add the zucchini to the prepared couscous with a handful of freshly chopped mint.

baked *eggplant* with *garlic* and *tomatoes*

This is a traditional, summery Turkish dish called "imam bayildi." The eggplants are halved, filled with simple ingredients, and baked slowly until they are soft and bursting with flavor. This is easy enough for a casual dinner at home (remembering that the eggplants will need 45 minutes in the oven) but also special enough for when you have friends round.

Heat half the olive oil in a large skillet, add the eggplants, and shallow-fry, turning them over until light golden on both sides, about 10–15 minutes. (Fry in batches if your skillet is too small.) Remove and drain on paper towels. Arrange the pieces side by side in an ovenproof dish and season with salt and pepper.

Preheat the oven to 375°F.

To make the stuffing, heat the remaining olive oil in a saucepan, add the onion, and sauté gently until it starts to color. Add the garlic and cumin and fry for 2–3 minutes. Add the tomatoes, oregano, some salt and pepper, the sugar, and ⅔ cup water, then cover with a lid and cook for 15 minutes, stirring occasionally.

Stir in the parsley, then divide the stuffing into 4 equal portions. Pile each portion along the length of each eggplant half. Add the diluted tomato paste to the base of the dish and cook in the preheated oven for 45 minutes, basting the eggplant once during cooking. Serve hot or warm.

serves
4

⅔ cup olive oil

2 medium eggplants, rinsed and halved lengthwise

salt and black pepper

Stuffing

1 onion, finely chopped

2 garlic cloves, crushed

½ teaspoon ground cumin

14 oz. ripe tomatoes, chopped

2 teaspoons dried oregano

½ teaspoon sugar

2 tablespoons freshly chopped parsley

2 teaspoons tomato paste, diluted with ⅔ cup hot water

roasted early fall *vegetables* with *chickpeas*

12 small mushrooms

2 ripe tomatoes, halved

1 red bell pepper, seeded and cut into strips

1 yellow bell pepper, seeded and cut into strips

1 red onion, cut into wedges

1 small fennel bulb, sliced into thin wedges

1 whole garlic bulb, broken into individual cloves but left unpeeled

2 teaspoons salt

2 tablespoons olive oil

14-oz. can chickpeas, drained and rinsed

2 thyme or rosemary sprigs

serves 4

This is no-fuss cooking at its best. Throw a few tasty vegetables into a roomy roasting pan, chuck in a lot of garlic and a can of chickpeas—for protein—and you have yourself the makings of a great Saturday supper. The garlic cloves turn soft and sweet in their skins so make sure you squeeze out and enjoy the flesh. It's delicious! Serve this winning meal with couscous, which always seems to like being with slow-roasted Mediterranean veg.

Preheat the oven to 350°F.

Put the mushrooms, tomatoes, bell peppers, onion, fennel, and garlic bulbs in a large roasting pan. Sprinkle the salt evenly over the vegetables and drizzle with the oil. Toss well to coat. Roast in the preheated oven for 1 hour.

Remove the roasting pan from the oven and turn the vegetables. Add the chickpeas and thyme sprigs. Return the pan to the oven and roast for a further 30 minutes, until the edges of the vegetables are just starting to blacken and char. Serve with couscous, if you like.

orange *vegetable* and *scallion* pilau

This technique of cooking rice is Middle Eastern in origin but it has spread far and wide—similar rice dishes can be found in European, Asian, Latin American, Caribbean, and Indian cuisines, and it is known by many names including pilaf, pilav, and pulao. It's one of those surprisingly satisfying recipes that you will come back to again and again—perfect bowl food for gobbling up on the couch in front of the TV.

serves
4

2 tablespoons olive oil

1 onion, chopped

2 garlic cloves, chopped

2 inches fresh ginger, peeled and finely chopped

1 large red chile, finely chopped

1 teaspoon ground coriander

1 teaspoon ground cumin

1 teaspoon turmeric

½ cup slivered almonds

1½ cups basmati rice

1 carrot, cut into large chunks

7 oz. pumpkin or squash, peeled, seeded and cut into wedges

1 small sweet potato, cut into thick half-circles

juice of 1 lime

a handful of cilantro, freshly chopped

Put the oil in a heavy-based saucepan set over high heat. Add the onion, garlic, ginger, and chile and cook for 5 minutes, stirring often. Add the spices and almonds and cook for a further 5 minutes, until the spices become aromatic and look very dark in the pan.

Add the rice and cook for a minute, stirring well to coat the rice in the spices. Add the carrot, pumpkin, and sweet potato to the pan. Pour in 2½ cups water and stir well, loosening any grains of rice that are stuck to the bottom of the pan. Bring to a boil, then reduce the heat to low, cover with a tight-fitting lid, and cook for 25 minutes, stirring occasionally.

Add the lime juice and cilantro, stir well to combine, and serve.

broccoli and *lemon* risotto

4 cups vegetable stock

4 tablespoons unsalted butter

1 tablespoon olive oil

8 shallots, finely chopped

2 garlic cloves, crushed

1½ cups risotto rice

¼ cup white wine

9 oz. purple sprouting broccoli, chopped, or broccoli florets

1 small red bell pepper, seeded and diced

1½ cups grated Parmesan

grated peel of 2 lemons

a handful of parsley, freshly chopped

salt and black pepper

serves 4

Risottos are ideal vegetarian fare. Make sure you buy real risotto rice, and don't skimp on the Parmesan or white wine (you can always enjoy the rest of the wine with your meal!) —these are the things that make a risotto so tasty. Purple sprouting broccoli is what you really want in this recipe—it has a delicious nutty flavor—but don't worry if you can't find it. Just use broccoli instead.

Put the stock in a large saucepan. Heat until almost boiling, then reduce the heat until barely simmering to keep it hot.

Heat the butter and oil in a large saucepan over medium heat. Add the shallots and cook for 1–2 minutes, until softened but not browned. Add the garlic and mix well.

Add the rice and stir, using a wooden spoon, until the grains are well coated and glistening, about 1 minute. Pour in the wine and stir until it has been completely absorbed.

Add 1 ladle of hot stock and simmer, stirring until it has been absorbed. Repeat. After 10 minutes, add the broccoli and bell pepper. Continue to add the stock at intervals and cook as before, for a further 8–10 minutes, until the liquid has been absorbed and the broccoli and rice are tender but still firm (al dente).

Add the Parmesan, lemon peel, parsley, and some salt and pepper. Mix well. Remove from the heat, cover, and let rest for 2 minutes.

Spoon into bowls and serve immediately.

roasted *butternut squash* risotto

This is quite a special risotto. It doesn't need much effort, or even any fancy ingredients, but it looks and tastes so good that you think it must have required a lot of work. In fact, the secret to its success is roasting the squash first, which brings out its sweetness, while the pumpkin seeds add a spicy crunch.

serves
2

1 lb. butternut squash, peeled, seeded, and diced

3 tablespoons olive oil

1½ teaspoons hot red pepper flakes

2 tablespoons pumpkin seeds

3½ cups vegetable stock

1 small onion, finely chopped

¾ cup risotto rice

½ cup white wine

½ cup grated Parmesan

salt and black pepper

crème fraîche or sour cream, to serve

Preheat the oven to 450°F.

Put the butternut squash in a small roasting pan with 1 tablespoon of the olive oil and ½ teaspoon of the pepper flakes and season well. Toss the squash in the seasoned oil until it is evenly coated. Roast in the preheated oven for about 20 minutes, or until soft and golden. (Use a large spoon to turn the squash at regular intervals while it is cooking.)

Heat 1 tablespoon of the remaining olive oil in a small skillet and toast the pumpkin seeds with the remaining pepper flakes for about 1–2 minutes until lightly browned. Set aside until needed.

While the squash is cooking in the oven, make the risotto. Put the stock in a saucepan. Heat until almost boiling, then reduce the heat until barely simmering to keep it hot.

Pour the remaining oil into a saucepan and gently fry the onion over medium heat for about 1 minute, or until softened. Add the rice, stir for 2–3 minutes, then add the wine and simmer until reduced by half. Add another ladleful of hot stock. Let the risotto continue to simmer gently, adding another ladleful or two of stock each time the liquid has been absorbed into the rice. Stir, almost continuously, until the rice has absorbed all the stock.

Once the rice is cooked and tender, stir in the roasted butternut squash and Parmesan and season to taste. Serve immediately, topped with a little crème fraîche and sprinkled with the toasted pumpkin seeds.

farmers' risotto

serves
4

4 cups vegetable stock

4 tablespoons unsalted butter

1 tablespoon olive oil

8 shallots, finely chopped

1 garlic clove, crushed

1½ cups risotto rice

⅓ cup white wine

1 small zucchini, finely chopped

2–3 firm tomatoes, seeded and finely chopped

2 oz. green beans, finely chopped

1 small leek, thinly sliced

1½ cups grated Parmesan

2 tablespoons light cream

a small handful of parsley, freshly chopped

a small handful of basil, leaves torn

salt and black pepper

When you can't decide what to cook, look to the vegetables in your fridge for inspiration—they're usually suitable for a risotto. This one is easy to make and you can use any vegetable you like. Just remember to cut them into neat, equal-size pieces for even cooking.

Put the stock in a saucepan. Heat until almost boiling, then reduce the heat until barely simmering to keep it hot.

Heat the butter and oil in a large saucepan over medium heat. Add the shallots and cook for 1–2 minutes, until softened but not browned. Add the garlic and mix well.

Add the rice and stir until the grains are well coated and glistening, about 1 minute. Pour in the wine and stir until it has been completely absorbed.

Add 1 ladle of hot stock and simmer, stirring until it has been absorbed. Repeat. After 10 minutes, add all the vegetables and mix well. Continue to add stock at intervals and cook as before, for a further 8–10 minutes, until the liquid has been absorbed and the vegetables and rice are tender but still firm (al dente).

Mix in the Parmesan, cream, herbs, and some salt and pepper. Remove from the heat, cover, and let rest for 2 minutes before serving.

mushroom risotto

Any kind of fresh wild mushroom will make this taste
wonderful—but wild mushrooms can be very expensive, so the
cheat's trick is to use a mixture of cultivated mushrooms, plus
a small amount of dried porcini mushrooms. Dried porcini are
one of those useful pantry ingredients that add flavor to many
recipes. You need to soak them in hot water before using, to
rejuvenate them.

serves
6

1 oz. dried porcini

3 cups assorted mushrooms

4 cups vegetable stock

1 stick unsalted butter

1 large onion, finely chopped

2 garlic cloves, finely
chopped

1 teaspoon dried thyme

⅓ cup white wine

2⅓ cups risotto rice

¾ cup grated Parmesan,
plus extra to serve

salt and black pepper

Put the dried porcini mushrooms in a small bowl, cover with warm water,
and set aside for 20 minutes. Drain and chop.

Clean the fresh, assorted mushrooms with a soft cloth and trim the stems
if necessary. Chop the larger mushrooms in half.

Put the stock in a saucepan and keep at a gentle simmer. Melt the butter
in a large, heavy saucepan and add the onion and garlic. Cook gently for
10 minutes until softened but not browned. Stir in the mushrooms and herbs,
then cook over medium heat for 3 minutes to heat through. Pour in the wine
and stir until it has been completely absorbed. Stir in the rice and fry with
the onion and mushrooms until slightly opaque.

Begin adding the stock, a large ladle at a time, stirring until each ladle has
been absorbed by the rice. Continue until the rice is tender and creamy, but
the grains still firm (al dente), about 18–20 minutes.

Taste and season well with salt and pepper. Stir in the Parmesan, cover, and
let rest for a couple of minutes before serving. Serve immediately with extra
grated Parmesan.

country-style risotto

4 cups vegetable stock

2 tablespoons olive oil

2 garlic cloves, crushed

4 oz. pumpkin flesh, diced

2 ripe plum tomatoes, seeded and chopped

⅓ cup peas (fresh or frozen)

10 green beans, chopped

1 small zucchini, chopped

7 tablespoons unsalted butter

8 shallots, finely chopped

1 carrot, finely chopped

2 celery ribs, finely chopped

a handful of parsley, freshly chopped

1½ cups risotto rice

½ cup white wine

1½ cups grated Parmesan

salt and black pepper

serves
4

This is the kind of hearty risotto you want on a cold wintry evening. Cook the vegetables in a separate pan (to retain their individual flavors and textures), then add them to the risotto. If you don't want to use pumpkin, or it's not in season, you can use broccoli instead.

Put the stock in a saucepan. Heat until almost boiling, then reduce the heat until barely simmering to keep it hot.

Heat 1 tablespoon of the olive oil in a skillet and add the garlic, pumpkin, tomatoes, peas, green beans, and zucchini. Cook until just tender, about 8 minutes, then remove and set aside.

Heat half the butter and the remaining oil in a large saucepan over medium heat. Add the shallots, carrot, celery, and parsley and cook for 1–2 minutes, until softened but not browned.

Add the rice and stir until the grains are well coated and glistening, about 1 minute. Pour in the wine and stir until it has been completely absorbed.

Add 1 ladle of hot stock and simmer, stirring until it has been absorbed. Continue to add the stock at intervals and cook as before, until the liquid has been absorbed and the rice is tender but still firm (al dente), about 18–20 minutes. Reserve the last ladle of stock.

Add the reserved stock and cooked vegetables, and some salt and pepper. Mix well. Stir in the Parmesan and remaining butter. Mix well. Remove from the heat, cover, and let rest for 2 minutes before serving.

spinach risotto with arugula and roasted tomatoes

This simple risotto makes the most of young spinach and peppery arugula, but watercress makes a good alternative if you can't find arugula. Roasting the tomatoes first means that this is not a last-minute risotto, but is does make the tomotoes lovely and sweet, so it's well worth the extra time.

serves
4

1 lb. cherry tomatoes

¼ cup olive oil

4 cups vegetable stock

a dash of soy sauce

6 tablespoons unsalted butter

1 onion, finely chopped

1½ cups risotto rice

⅔ cups white wine

6 oz. young spinach leaves

2 oz. arugula

salt and black pepper

grated Parmesan, to serve

Preheat the oven to 400°F.

Put the tomatoes in a roasting pan and drizzle with olive oil. Mix well to coat, then season with salt and pepper. Roast in the preheated oven for about 20 minutes or until slightly collapsed with the skins beginning to brown. Remove from the oven and set aside.

Put the stock and soy sauce in a saucepan. Heat until almost boiling, then reduce the heat until barely simmering to keep it hot.

Melt half the butter in a large, heavy saucepan and add the onion. Cook gently for 10 minutes until softened but not browned. Add the rice and stir until well coated with the butter and heated through. Pour in the wine and stir until it has been completely absorbed. Remove from the heat.

Return the risotto to the heat, warm through, and begin adding the stock, a large ladle at a time, stirring gently until each ladle has been almost absorbed into the rice. Continue until the rice is tender and creamy, but the grains still firm (al dente), about 18–20 minutes.

Just before the risotto is cooked, stir in the spinach and arugula. Taste and season well with salt and pepper and beat in the remaining butter and the Parmesan. You may like to add a little more hot stock to the risotto at this stage to loosen it.

Cover and let rest for 2 minutes. Fold in the tomatoes and their juices then serve immediately.

tomato risotto

4 cups vegetable stock

4 tablespoons unsalted butter

1 tablespoon olive oil

8 shallots, finely chopped

2 garlic cloves, crushed

1½ cups risotto rice

8 firm tomatoes, seeded and coarsely chopped

1½ cups grated Parmesan

a large handful of basil, leaves torn

salt and black pepper

serves
4

Try to find really tasty tomatoes for this risotto—since they are the main ingredient, they need to be full of flavor otherwise the risotto will end up bland. The combination of tomatoes, basil, and Parmesan is deliciously Italian.

Put the stock in a saucepan. Heat until almost boiling, then reduce the heat until barely simmering to keep it hot.

Heat the butter and oil in a large saucepan over medium heat. Add the shallots and cook for 1–2 minutes, until softened but not browned. Add the garlic and mix well.

Add the rice and stir until the grains are well coated and glistening, about 1 minute. Pour in the wine and stir until it has been completely absorbed.

Add 1 ladle of hot stock and simmer, stirring until it has been absorbed. Repeat. After 10 minutes, add the tomatoes. Continue to add the stock at intervals and cook as before, for a further 8–10 minutes, until the liquid has been absorbed and the tomatoes and rice are tender but still firm (al dente). Reserve the last ladle of stock.

Stir in the reserved stock, Parmesan, basil, and some salt and pepper. Remove from the heat, cover, and let rest for 2 minutes before serving.

risotto with *lemon* and *mint*

Sometimes you don't want a heavy risotto packed with ingredients. This is a wonderfully light and fresh-tasting option with the sunshine flavors of lemon and mint. It requires so few ingredients that it's good if you unexpectedly get hungry friends round for dinner.

serves
4

Put the stock in a saucepan. Heat until almost boiling, then reduce the heat until barely simmering to keep it hot.

Heat the butter and oil in a large saucepan over medium heat. Add the shallots and cook for 1–2 minutes, until softened but not browned. Add the garlic and mix well.

Add the rice and stir until the grains are well coated and glistening, about 1 minute. Pour in the wine and stir until it has been completely absorbed.

Add 1 ladle of hot stock and simmer, stirring until it has been absorbed. Continue to add the stock at intervals and cook as before, until the liquid has been absorbed and the rice is tender but firm (al dente), about 18–20 minutes.

Stir in the Parmesan, lemon peel, cream, mint, and some salt and pepper. Remove from the heat, cover, and let rest for 2 minutes before serving.

4 cups vegetable stock

4 tablespoons unsalted butter

1 tablespoon olive oil

8 shallots, finely chopped

1 garlic clove, crushed

1½ cups risotto rice

⅛ cup white wine

1½ cups grated Parmesan

grated peel of 3 lemons

2 tablespoons light cream

a handful of mint, freshly chopped

salt and black pepper

vegetable burritos

serves 4

Q

14-oz. can chopped tomatoes

3 garlic cloves, crushed

1 tablespoon mild chili powder, or to taste

a pinch of dried oregano

1 tablespoon tomato paste

1 tablespoon olive oil

1 yellow bell pepper, seeded and sliced

1 green bell pepper, seeded and sliced

14-oz. can refried beans (or borlotti or pinto beans, rinsed, drained, and mashed)

4 soft flour or corn tortillas

3½ oz. cheddar, grated

2 tablespoons crème fraîche or sour cream

2 tablespoons freshly chopped cilantro

salt and black pepper

Salsa

½ large red onion

2 tomatoes

½ green chile, seeded and finely chopped

1 tablespoon lime juice

1 tablespoon freshly chopped mint

Everyone loves burritos! They're the perfect TV dinner but that doesn't mean they have to be bad for you. These are made with yellow and green bell peppers and freshly made tomato salsa, and the refried beans are high in fiber. If there's a meat-eater among you, you can easily pan-fry some strips of chicken breast for them to add to their burrito filling.

Put the tomatoes in a saucepan with the garlic, chili powder, oregano, and tomato paste. Bring to a boil, reduce the heat, and simmer for 10 minutes, until the mixture reduces slightly and begins to thicken.

Meanwhile, heat the oil in a separate saucepan. Add the bell peppers and sauté for about 5 minutes, until soft. Add the peppers to the tomato mixture.

Put the refried beans in another saucepan and heat gently, stirring frequently until piping hot.

To make the salsa, put all the ingredients in a small bowl and mix well.

Warm the tortillas according to the instructions on the package.

Put the tortillas on 4 serving plates. Spread each tortilla with a thick layer of refried beans, then 1 tablespoon of the tomato and pepper mixture, 2 tablespoons of cheese, 1 tablespoon of the salsa, and ½ tablespoon crème fraîche. Sprinkle with cilantro, fold, and serve immediately.

huevos rancheros

serves 4

These "ranch eggs" are so brilliant because you can eat them at any time of day! They're often served up for breakfast or brunch, but they make an excellent choice for dinner or lunch too, because they're satisfying and filling. Unlike the Vegetable Burritos on page 148, the refried beans are homemade—you just need a can of pinto or cannellini beans and cheese to make your own simple version. If you want to serve the huevos rancheros with a spoonful of guacamole or sour cream, that's a great idea, too.

Heat 1 tablespoon of the oil in a large skillet over medium heat, then add the chile, half the garlic, and a pinch of salt and fry for 1–2 minutes, until softened. Add the tomatoes and cook gently for about 20 minutes.

Heat the remaining oil in a small saucepan, add the remaining garlic, and heat through for 20 seconds, until just browning. Add the beans, then using a potato masher, coarsely mash the beans and stir in plenty of salt and pepper and the cheddar.

Stir the lime juice and cilantro into the tomato sauce. Make 4 holes in the sauce and crack an egg into each one. Cook for 3 minutes until set. Cover with the lid for the last 30 seconds just to firm up the whites. Keep warm until needed.

Meanwhile, heat a skillet over medium heat. Cook the tortillas for 1 minute on each side, until golden and hot. Transfer to 4 plates and spread the beans over the tortillas. Top with tomato salsa and the eggs. Serve with lime wedges and guacamole or sour cream if you like.

3 tablespoons vegetable oil

1 green chile, seeded and finely chopped

2 garlic cloves, crushed

1 lb. tomatoes, cut into slim wedges

14-oz. can pinto or cannellini beans

½ cup grated cheddar

juice of 1 lime, plus extra lime wedges to serve

a handful of cilantro, freshly chopped

4 eggs

4 soft flour or corn tortillas

salt and black pepper

mozzarella-topped *herby vegetable* loaf

 serves 3–4

This recipe is a bit like a veggie version of meatballs in tomato sauce. Eat it as it is or serve it with a little pasta or with new potatoes and peas or broccoli on the side.

8 oz. carrots, grated

1 red onion, finely chopped

2 garlic cloves, crushed

3 celery ribs, finely chopped

4 oz. mushrooms, sliced

1 small zucchini, sliced

1 tablespoon freshly chopped parsley

2 tablespoons freshly chopped cilantro

⅔ cup grated cheddar

2 eggs

1 cup whole-wheat flour

1½ cups grated mozzarella

Sauce

3 tablespoons olive oil

½ onion, sliced

1 garlic clove, crushed

2 x 14-oz. cans chopped tomatoes

1 teaspoon sugar

salt and black pepper

a 1-lb. loaf pan, lined with baking parchment

Preheat the oven to 350°F.

Mix the carrots, onion, garlic, celery, mushrooms, zucchini, parsley, cilantro, cheddar, eggs, and flour in a large bowl. Spoon the mixture into the prepared loaf pan and bake in the preheated oven for 1 hour.

Meanwhile, to make the sauce, heat the olive oil in a saucepan. Add the onion and garlic, cover with a lid, and sweat over gentle heat until soft and pale golden.

Add the canned tomatoes (with all the juice) to the onion mixture. Stir in the sugar and season to taste.

Cook, uncovered, for about 30 minutes, or until the tomato softens.

Remove the loaf from the oven and let stand for 5 minutes. Preheat the broiler to hot.

Tip the loaf out onto a plate and slice. Put the slices into a shallow, ovenproof dish. Pour over the tomato sauce and sprinkle with the mozzarella. Broil for 4–5 minutes, or until the cheese is bubbling and golden. Serve immediately.

rice and *bean* burgers

There's something really satisfying about making your own burgers, especially when the finished product is superior to anything you might find in the shops. This recipe takes a little longer than you might expect but you will be rewarded with at least 5 meals (2 burgers per meal) for your labor. Put any leftover burgers in the freezer before you cook them and take them out to defrost thoroughly as and when you need them.

makes
10

1¾ cups brown rice (not parboiled variety)

2 tablespoons Worcestershire sauce

1 onion, chopped

2 garlic cloves, crushed

6½ oz. canned cannellini beans, drained and rinsed

6½ oz. canned red kidney beans, drained and rinsed

½ cup bread crumbs

1 egg, beaten

1 cup grated cheddar

2 tablespoons freshly chopped thyme

1 small green bell pepper, seeded and chopped

1 large carrot, coarsely grated

flour or cornmeal, for coating

2–3 tablespoons safflower oil

salt and black pepper

salad greens and relish, to serve (optional)

Cook the rice according to the instructions on the package, allowing it to slightly overcook so that it is soft. Drain the rice, transfer it to a large bowl, and reserve.

Put 2 tablespoons water and the Worcestershire sauce in a skillet, add the onion and garlic, and cook until softened, about 8 minutes.

Put the onions, garlic, cooked rice, beans, bread crumbs, egg, cheese, and thyme in a blender or food processor. Add plenty of salt and pepper, then blend until combined. Alternatively, you can mash everything roughly in a bowl with a potato masher. Add the bell pepper and grated carrot and mix well. Refrigerate the mixture for 1½ hours, or until quite firm.

Shape the mixture into 10 burgers, using wet hands if the mixture sticks. Coat them in flour or cornmeal and refrigerate for a further 30 minutes.

Heat the oil in a skillet and fry the burgers for 3–4 minutes on each side, or until piping hot. Serve with salad greens and relish.

Variation Add 1–2 seeded finely chopped chiles to give an extra bite and 3 finely chopped celery ribs to add some crunch, if you like. Replace the thyme with freshly chopped cilantro.

spiced *falafel* burgers

1¼ cups dried chickpeas (or use 14-oz. can chickpeas and skip the soaking step)

1 small onion, finely chopped

2 garlic cloves, crushed

½ handful of parsley, freshly chopped

½ handful of cilantro, freshly chopped

2 teaspoons ground coriander

½ teaspoon baking powder

4 hero rolls

a handful of salad greens

2 tomatoes, diced

salt and black pepper

safflower oil, for shallow frying

Yogurt sauce

½ cup thick plain yogurt

1 tablespoon tahini (sesame seed paste)

1 garlic clove, crushed

½ tablespoon lemon juice

1 tablespoon olive oil

 makes 8

Falafels are Egyptian bean patties traditionally served in pita bread with salad greens and hummus. Here they make a great burger filling with a yogurt dressing. You will need to use dried chickpeas and soak them overnight before starting the burgers (although you could cheat and use canned chickpeas instead). You will also need a blender or food processor for this recipe.

Put the dried chickpeas in a bowl and add cold water to cover by at least 5 inches. Let soak overnight.

The next day, drain the chickpeas well, transfer to a blender or food processor, and blend until coarsely ground. Add the onion, garlic, parsley, cilantro, ground coriander, baking powder, and some salt and pepper and blend until very smooth. Transfer to a bowl, cover, and refrigerate for 30 minutes.

To make the yogurt sauce, put the yogurt, tahini, garlic, lemon juice, and olive oil in a bowl and whisk until smooth. Season to taste with salt and pepper and set aside until required.

Using wet hands, shape the chickpea mixture into 8 medium patties. Heat a shallow layer of oil in a skillet, add the patties, and fry for 3 minutes on each side until golden and cooked through. Drain on paper towels.

Cut the rolls in half and fill with 2 patties, yogurt sauce, salad greens, and diced tomato. Serve hot.

chunky eggplant burgers

chunky *eggplant* burgers

The smoky taste of grilled eggplant and the basil pesto give these burgers a distinctive Mediterranean flavor. You could replace the sliced tomatoes with semi-dried tomatoes if you like.

Preheat the broiler to high.

Cut the eggplant into ½-inch slices. Put the oil, vinegar, garlic, and some salt and pepper in a bowl. Whisk to mix, then brush over the eggplant slices. Arrange them on a broiler pan or in a baking dish and broil for 3–4 minutes on each side until charred and softened.

Lightly toast the rolls and top with a slice of eggplant. Spread with pesto, add another slice of eggplant, then add a slice of tomato and mozzarella. Drizzle with more pesto, then top with a few arugula leaves. Put the tops on the rolls and serve hot.

makes
4

Q

1 large eggplant, about 1½ lbs.

¼ cup olive oil

1 tablespoon balsamic vinegar

1 garlic clove, crushed

4 soft bread rolls, halved

2 beefsteak tomatoes, thickly sliced

8 oz. mozzarella, sliced

a handful of arugula

salt and black pepper

pesto, to serve

curried *sweet potato* burgers

You can either add some lime pickle and plain yogurt to these nutty burgers or serve them rolled in warm chapatti bread. Be aware that you will need to refrigerate the burgers for 30 minutes before cooking.

Put the bulgur wheat in a heatproof bowl, add boiling water to cover by 1 inch, and set aside to soak for 20 minutes until tender. Drain well.

Meanwhile, steam the potatoes for 10–15 minutes until cooked. Drain well and mash with a potato masher. Heat the olive oil in a skillet and fry the onion, garlic, and curry powder for 10 minutes until the onion is softened.

Put the bulgur wheat, mashed potato, onion mixture, almonds, cilantro, egg, flour, and some salt and pepper in a bowl. Work together with your hands until evenly mixed. Cover and refrigerate for 30 minutes. Using wet hands, divide the mixture into 8 portions and shape into patties.

Heat a shallow layer of olive oil in a skillet, add the patties, and fry gently for 3–4 minutes on each side until golden and heated through. Cut the buns in half, toast, and fill with 2 patties, salad greens, cucumber slices, and mango chutney. Serve hot.

makes
4

½ cup bulgur wheat

1 lb. sweet potatoes, cubed

1½ tablespoons olive oil, plus extra for shallow frying

1 small onion, finely chopped

1 garlic clove, crushed

1 tablespoon curry powder

½ cup blanched almonds, finely chopped

2 tablespoons freshly chopped cilantro

1 egg, lightly beaten

¼ cup all-purpose flour

4 burger buns

a handful of salad greens

2 inches cucumber, sliced

¼ cup mango chutney

salt and black pepper

greek omelet

serves
2

This is not a traditional recipe. It's been named a "Greek omelet" simply because it contains Greek-inspired ingredients, many of which can probably be found at your local store. This omelet is fast to make, nice to look at, and easy to eat, so you might find yourself cooking it often. Serve it hot or cold, with crusty bread or pita. The recipe serves 2 as an entrée or 4 as a snack or appetizer.

olive oil, for frying

1 cup cherry tomatoes, halved

4–5 bottled marinated peppers (hot ones, if you like them!)

3 scallions, sliced

⅓ cup pitted black olives, sliced

4 oz. feta

a small handful of parsley, freshly chopped

6 large eggs

salt and black pepper

Salad

8 oz. mixed greens

1 tablespoon lemon juice

¼ cup olive oil

Preheat the oven to 400°F.

Drizzle a little oil into a large, round, ovenproof dish. Arrange the tomatoes, peppers, scallions, and olives equally around the dish. Crumble in the feta, then grind black pepper over the top. Sprinkle with parsley.

Put the eggs in a separate bowl, beat well, and season with a good pinch of salt. Pour over the ingredients in the dish. Bake in the preheated oven until puffed and just golden around the edges, 15–20 minutes.

To make the salad, put the greens in a bowl, add the lemon juice, oil, and some salt and pepper. Toss well, taste, and adjust the seasoning with more salt and pepper if necessary. Serve with the omelet cut into wedges—hot, warm, or at room temperature.

sweet potato and *brie* tortilla

Buy deep orange sweet potatoes to achieve the best effect for this colorful tortilla. To melt the Brie, the tortilla is finished in the oven, so use a skillet with a heatproof handle.

serves
2–3

2 medium sweet potatoes, about 1 lb., cut into chunks

¼ cup olive or safflower oil

1 onion, halved lengthwise and sliced

5 large eggs

1 garlic clove, crushed

4 oz. Brie

salt and black pepper

Preheat the oven to 400°F.

Put the potatoes and 2 tablespoons of the oil in a roasting pan and toss to coat. Roast in the preheated oven for 15 minutes, then add the onion and mix well. Roast in the oven for a further 20 minutes, or until the potatoes and onion are tender.

Break the eggs into a large bowl and whisk briefly with a fork. Stir in the garlic and some salt and pepper. Add the cooked potatoes and onions and mix gently.

Heat the remaining oil in a small skillet. Pour the tortilla mixture into the skillet and cook over medium-low heat for 6–8 minutes, or until it has set around the edges and is lightly browned underneath.

Slice the Brie and arrange on top of the tortilla. Transfer the skillet to the preheated oven for 5 minutes, or until the Brie has melted and the top of the tortilla has set. Serve hot or warm, cut into wedges.

roasted *vegetable* tortilla

 serves 3–4

1 red onion, cut into wedges

1 red bell pepper, seeded and cut into thick strips

1 leek, thickly sliced

4 oz. butternut squash, peeled, seeded, and cubed

6 sprigs of thyme

2 garlic cloves, unpeeled

3 tablespoons olive or safflower oil

6 large eggs

salt and black pepper

There's nothing quite like the grilled flavor of roasted vegetables; as a tortilla filling they make a delicious alternative to the more traditional potato. You can roast the vegetables up to 24 hours in advance and keep chilled until you are ready to make the tortilla, but allow a little extra time to cook the tortilla because the vegetables will be cold. The tortilla is finished under the broiler so use a skillet with a heatproof handle.

Preheat the oven to 400°F.

Put the onion, bell pepper, leek, and squash in large roasting pan. Sprinkle with thyme and some salt and pepper. Bury the garlic cloves under the vegetables and sprinkle with 2 tablespoons of the oil. Roast in the preheated oven for 20 minutes. Turn the vegetables over and roast in the oven for a further 10 minutes.

Remove from the oven and let cool for 5 minutes. Remove the soft flesh from the roasted garlic and discard the skins. Discard the thyme stalks, removing any leaves still attached.

Break the eggs into a large bowl, add some salt and pepper, and whisk briefly with a fork. Add the vegetables and mix gently.

Heat the remaining oil in a medium skillet. Add the tortilla mixture and cook over medium-low heat for about 10 minutes or until the bottom is golden brown and the top almost set.

Slide under a preheated broiler to finish cooking or put a plate over the top of the skillet and invert so the tortilla falls onto the plate. Slide back into the skillet and cook for 2–3 minutes. Let stand for 5 minutes to settle. Serve hot or at room temperature, cut into wedges.

zucchini, potato, and *onion* tortilla

1¼ lbs. potatoes, cut horizontally into thin slices

2 tablespoons olive oil

2 onions, halved lengthwise and cut into thin slices

2 zucchini, diced

6 large eggs

salt and black pepper

 serves 4–6

This light lunch or dinner ticks all the right boxes. It contains everyday ingredients, is simple to make, and combines a healthy balance of protein and carbohydrates. Serve with a watercress and tomato salad and crusty bread. The tortilla is finished under the broiler so use a skillet with a heatproof handle.

Cook the potatoes in boiling salted water for about 6 minutes until tender. Drain in a colander and cool under cold running water, then set aside.

Heat 1 tablespoon of the oil in a large skillet over medium-low heat. Add the onions and sauté, covered, for 10 minutes, stirring frequently, until softened but not browned. Add the zucchini and fry for another 3 minutes.

Meanwhile, lightly beat the eggs in a large bowl and season to taste. Add the cooked onions, zucchini, and potatoes and turn until the vegetables are well coated in the eggs.

Heat the remaining oil in the skillet. Remove the skillet from the heat and carefully pour the egg mixture into it. Make sure the vegetables are evenly distributed in the skillet, pressing them down into the egg.

Preheat the broiler to medium.

Return the skillet to the stove and cook the tortilla for 6 minutes, until the bottom is set and slightly golden. To cook the top, slide the skillet under the broiler and cook gently for 6–7 minutes, or until the egg is cooked. Alternatively, put a plate over the top of the skillet and invert so the tortilla falls onto the plate. Slide back into the skillet and cook for 2–3 minutes.

Allow the tortilla to cool slightly before cutting into wedges.

asian-style *tofu* omelet

This omelet has a distinctly Asian feel, with creamy cubes of tofu replacing the more traditional cheese.

serves
4

Q

Put the oil in a large skillet with a heatproof handle over high heat. Add the shallots, broccoli, and mushrooms and stir-fry for 3–4 minutes, until the mushrooms are soft and the broccoli turns bright green. Add the spinach and cook until just wilted. Add the soy sauce and stir. Arrange the tofu evenly over the vegetables.

Preheat the broiler to high.

Meanwhile, lightly beat the eggs and season to taste. Pour into the skillet and cook over high heat until the edges puffed. Place the skillet under the broiler and cook until golden and firm on top. Let cool a little before serving.

1 tablespoon olive oil

2 shallots, sliced

8 oz. tenderstem broccoli, chopped into small pieces

7 oz. shiitake mushrooms

2 oz. baby spinach leaves

2 teaspoons light soy sauce

10 oz. firm tofu, cubed

8 eggs

salt and white or black pepper

broccoli and *potato* frittata

The frittata is Italy's version of a flat, open-faced omelet. Ideally it should be cooked slowly, only lightly colored and still slightly moist when served. Try to find really small waxy potatoes for this frittata—they are creamy and yellow and sweeter than most larger varieties, and particularly good with tenderstem broccoli. Tenderstem broccoli is part broccoli and part Chinese chard and can be added to stir-fries, pastas, and salads. The frittata is finished under the broiler so use a skillet with a heatproof handle.

serves
4

8 small waxy potatoes, quartered

1 cup vegetable stock

¼ cup olive oil

8 oz. tenderstem broccoli, trimmed and halved lengthwise

1 red onion, thinly sliced

8 eggs

1 cup grated Parmesan

mixed green salad, to serve

Put the potatoes in a large skillet and pour over the stock. Put the skillet over high heat and bring the stock to a boil. Boil for 10 minutes, turning the potatoes often, until almost all the stock has been absorbed.

Add the olive oil, broccoli, and onion to the skillet and cook for 1 minute, turning the vegetables to coat in the oil. Cover and cook for 2–3 minutes, to soften the broccoli.

Preheat the broiler to high.

Lightly beat the eggs with half of the Parmesan and pour over the vegetables. Cover the skillet and cook over medium heat for 8–10 minutes, until the eggs look set.

Sprinkle over the remaining cheese, then place under the broiler and cook until the top of the frittata is golden. Alternatively, put a plate over the top of the skillet and invert so the frittata falls onto the plate. Slide back into the skillet and cook for 2–3 minutes.

Let cool slightly before removing from the skillet. Cut into wedges and serve with a mixed green salad.

feta, tomato, and *herb* omelet

5 large eggs

2 tablespoons freshly chopped basil

1 tablespoon freshly chopped mint

3 scallions, finely chopped

2 tablespoons safflower oil

3 oz. feta, crumbled

8 cherry tomatoes, halved

salt and black pepper

You'll be surprised how tasty this omelet is, given how basic the ingredients and method are. It's really a simpler version of the Greek Omelet on page 160. All the flavor derives from the quality of the ingredients so if you can, buy your cherry tomatoes still on the vine—they taste so much better that way. This is the kind of recipe you want to have on standby when there are just two of you for dinner and you don't want to slave over anything too filling or complicated. The omelet is finished under the broiler so use a skillet with a heatproof handle.

Break the eggs into a bowl and whisk briefly with a fork. Season with salt and pepper, add 2 tablespoons water, the basil, mint, and scallions, and mix briefly.

Heat the oil in a small skillet. Pour in the egg mixture and cook over medium heat for 4–5 minutes, drawing the mixture from the sides to the center until the omelet is half cooked.

Preheat the broiler to medium.

Top with the feta and the tomato halves, cut side up, and cook for 2 minutes. Slide under the broiler and cook until light golden brown. Alternatively, put a plate over the top of the skillet and invert so the omelet falls onto the plate. Slide back into the skillet and cook for 2–3 minutes.

Slide onto a warmed plate and serve immediately.

easy speedy pizza

You can make your own pizza from scratch in half an hour. You can add anything you like as a topping—though this mixture is always popular.

makes
4

Preheat the oven to 400°F.

Sift the flour, sugar, baking soda, and salt into a large bowl. Stir in the dried herbs.

With your hand, make a hollow in the middle of the flour and pour in the buttermilk or the yogurt and milk mixture. Using one hand, start to mix the flour into the liquid, then gradually work all the flour into the mixture to make a soft and slightly sticky dough. If there are dry crumbs and it is hard to work all the flour into the dough, add 1 tablespoon of buttermilk or milk. If the dough is sticky and feels very wet, work in a little more flour.

When the dough comes together in a ball, tip it out of the bowl onto a work surface lightly sprinkled with flour. Work the ball of dough with both hands for 1 minute until it looks smooth.

Divide the dough into 4 equal pieces. Shape each piece into a neat ball. Flour your hands, then gently pat out each piece of the dough to a circle about 7 inches across. Set the circles slightly apart on the greased sheets.

To make the topping, put the chopped tomatoes in a bowl with the tomato paste, olive oil, herbs, garlic, and some salt and pepper. Mix well.

Spoon 2 tablespoons of the tomato topping in the middle of each pizza base. Spread over the pizza, leaving a 1-inch border of uncovered dough all around the edge. Arrange the mozzarella over the topping. Finally, top with as many extras as you like.

Bake the pizzas in the preheated oven until light golden and bubbling, about 15–18 minutes.

Let cool for a couple of minutes before serving.

3 cups all-purpose flour, plus extra for dusting

1 teaspoon sugar

1 teaspoon baking soda

1 teaspoon salt

½ teaspoon dried oregano or thyme

1¼ cups buttermilk or ¾ cup plain yogurt plus ¾ cup milk

Topping

14-oz. can chopped tomatoes

1 tablespoon tomato paste

1 tablespoon olive oil

1 teaspoon dried oregano or thyme

1 garlic clove, crushed

2 mozzarella balls, about 6 oz. each, sliced

salt and black pepper

Optional extras

green or black pitted olives, sliced red or green bell pepper, or mushrooms

2 large baking sheets, greased

food to impress

couscous with roast *squash, halloumi, dates,* and *pistachios*

It might sound unusual, but peppermint tea is great for fluffing up the grains of couscous and works well alongside the sweetness of squash and salty, squeaky halloumi. It is strong and minty, so it only needs a brief stint in hot water.

serves
4–6

1 lb. butternut squash or pumpkin, peeled, seeded, and cut into wedges

3 tablespoons olive oil

3 dried bay leaves

3 sprigs of thyme

4 garlic cloves, unpeeled

2 large dried chiles or 1 teaspoon hot red pepper flakes

8 oz. halloumi, cubed

3 tablespoons pistachios, shelled and chopped

2 peppermint tea bags

1¼ cups just-boiled water

1¼ cups couscous

4 oz. fresh dates, pitted and finely chopped

salt and black pepper

Preheat the oven to 400°F.

Put the squash in a roasting pan, drizzle with 2 tablespoons of the olive oil, and tuck in the bay leaves, thyme, garlic cloves, and chiles or pepper flakes. Roast in the preheated oven for 25 minutes, or until the squash is almost tender. Raise the oven temperature to 475°F. Add the halloumi and pistachios, drizzle with the remaining olive oil, and roast for a further 10 minutes, or until the halloumi is golden.

Meanwhile, put the peppermint tea bags in a heatproof pitcher or a teapot and pour over the hot water. Let steep for 1 minute, then discard the tea bags. Put the couscous and dates in a large bowl, season to taste, and pour over the hot tea. Cover with plastic wrap and leave for 5 minutes, or until the grains have swollen and absorbed all the tea.

Fluff up the couscous with a fork, stirring in about half the ingredients from the roasting pan at the same time, but leaving behind the whole chiles, if using. Spoon into 4–6 bowls and top with the remaining ingredients.

braised *fennel* with *polenta*

2 large fennel bulbs

¼ cup olive oil

1 onion, chopped

2 garlic cloves, chopped

1 small red chile, seeded and chopped

a handful of parsley, freshly chopped

2 tablespoons lemon juice

2 tablespoons white wine

2 cups vegetable stock

a handful of small, pitted black olives

Polenta

2 cups milk

4 cups vegetable stock

1¼ cups instant polenta

3 tablespoons butter

1 cup grated Pecorino or Parmesan

serves 4

Try to buy fennel with the feathery leaves intact, as these can be added to the final stages of a dish or used as a garnish. While smaller, tender bulbs can be eaten raw, the larger, tougher ones are perfect when braised, as here. The polenta—made creamy with milk, butter, and cheese—makes everything more filling and even tastier.

Cut about ¼ inch from the gnarly stem on the bottom of the fennel bulbs. Cut off the fronds (the feathery leaves), chop finely, and reserve. Cut off and discard all but about ¼ inch from the dark green stems. Thinly slice the remaining white fennel bulb lengthwise.

Put the oil in a heavy-based saucepan and set over high heat. Add the onions, garlic, and chile and cook for 2–3 minutes until softened. Add the parsley and fennel bulb and fronds and cook for 2–3 minutes, stirring often so that the fennel becomes coated in the oil. Add the lemon juice, wine, and stock and bring to a boil. Cover with a lid and turn the heat down to a low simmer for 20 minutes, stirring occasionally. Add the olives, remove the lid, and boil rapidly until there is only a little liquid left and the fennel is very soft and tender.

Meanwhile, to make the polenta, put the milk and stock in a saucepan and bring to a gentle simmer over medium heat. Slowly pour in the polenta in a steady stream and beat with a whisk until smooth. Reduce the heat to low and continue to beat for 2–3 minutes. When the mixture thickens, discard the whisk and use a wooden spoon. Add the butter and cheese and stir until melted into the polenta. Spoon some polenta onto serving plates, top with the braised fennel, and serve.

feta-stuffed bell peppers

feta-stuffed *bell peppers*

This healthy combination of bulgur wheat, sharp feta, and sweet bell peppers tastes divine.

Put the bulgur wheat in a bowl, cover with boiling water, and let stand for 30 minutes, until the grains are puffed and swollen. Drain, if necessary, and fluff with a fork to separate the grains.

Preheat the oven to 350°F.

Meanwhile, cut the bell peppers in half lengthwise and scrape out and discard the seeds and membranes. Leave the stalks intact so the peppers hold their shape. Transfer the peppers to an ovenproof dish.

Put the apple and lemon juice in a bowl and mix lightly. Add the drained bulgur wheat, feta, herbs, garlic, ginger, raisins, scallions, and oil. Season with salt and pepper and mix well. Divide the mixture between the halved peppers. Pour a little water in the dish around the peppers and cook in the preheated oven for 20–25 minutes, until the filling is piping hot.

serves 4

⅓ cup bulgur wheat

2 yellow bell peppers

2 orange bell peppers

1 red apple, cored and chopped

1 tablespoon lemon juice

5 oz. feta, crumbled

3 tablespoons freshly chopped mixed herbs, such as dill, basil, parsley, mint, and cilantro

2 garlic cloves, crushed

1 inch fresh ginger, peeled and finely grated

⅓ cup raisins

8 scallions, chopped

1–2 tablespoons olive oil

salt and black pepper

baked *goat cheese* on *toast*

Sometimes, only cheese on toast will do. But take some goat cheese and a couple of slices of really good bread, and you have the most decadent and irresistible grilled cheese imaginable.

serves 2

Preheat the oven to 400°F.

Put the goat cheese slices onto the prepared baking sheet, sprinkle with a little oil, dot with thyme leaves, and season with pepper. Bake in the preheated oven for 10–12 minutes until just starting to ooze and run.

Meanwhile, toast the bread and rub it with the garlic. When the cheese is ready, spread it onto the toasted bread and serve with a green salad.

4 thick slices of goat cheese with rind, 2 oz. per serving

1 tablespoon freshly chopped thyme

4 slices of bread, preferably sourdough

1 garlic clove, halved

green salad, to serve

black pepper

olive oil, for sprinkling

a baking sheet, lined with foil

baked *spinach* mornay

3 tablespoons butter

2 tablespoons all-purpose flour

3 cups milk

7 oz. Fontina (or a similar cheese, like Gruyère or Edam), cubed

1 onion, chopped

1 garlic clove, chopped

2 lbs. spinach leaves, chopped

½ teaspoon grated nutmeg

toasted and buttered bread, to serve (optional)

serves 6

This is really rich and ideally served with something doughy like the Upside-down Tomato Tart on page 205 or a simple green salad with a tangy vinaigrette. It is also a great brunch dish, perfect with poached eggs and hot buttered toast.

Preheat oven to 350°F.

Put 2 tablespoons of the butter in a saucepan over medium heat. When it is melted and sizzling, add the flour and cook for 1 minute, stirring constantly, until a thick paste forms.

Reduce the heat to low and slowly pour the milk into the pan, whisking constantly, until all the milk is incorporated and the mixture is smooth and lump-free. Add the cheese and stir until it has melted into the sauce. Set aside until needed.

Heat the remaining butter in a large skillet over high heat, add the onion and garlic, and cook for 2–3 minutes, until the onion has softened. Add the spinach, cover with a lid, and cook for 4–5 minutes, stirring often, until the spinach has wilted. Transfer the spinach to a large bowl. Pour in the cheese sauce and stir to combine.

Spoon the mixture into a large baking dish. Sprinkle the nutmeg over the top and bake in the preheated oven for 30 minutes until the top of the mornay is golden and bubbling. Serve on slices of toasted and buttered bread if you like.

eggplant, tomato, and *parmesan* gratin

serves 4

A gratin is usually a shallow dish of vegetables topped with bread crumbs or grated cheese and baked in the oven. This one is particularly pretty and bursting with flavor. Tomato halves are baked with briefly fried, sliced eggplant and Parmesan.

1 large eggplant

1 lb. very ripe tomatoes

about ⅔ cup olive oil

4 tablespoons freshly chopped basil

1¼ cups grated Parmesan

salt and black pepper

a shallow ovenproof dish, well greased

Cut the eggplant lengthwise into thin slices. Sprinkle with salt and let drain in a colander for 30 minutes. Rinse well and pat dry with paper towels. Cut the tomatoes in half through the middle.

Preheat the oven to 400°F.

Heat the oil in a large skillet and fry the eggplant in batches until deep golden brown. Drain on paper towels. Arrange a layer of eggplants in the prepared dish, then top with a layer of tomato halves, cut side up. Sprinkle with the chopped basil, salt, pepper, and half the Parmesan. Add another layer of eggplants, then sprinkle with the remaining Parmesan.

Bake in the preheated oven for 20–25 minutes, or until browned and bubbling on top. Let cool slightly and serve warm, or cool completely and serve as a salad.

mixed *vegetable* tian

A tian is a shallow baking dish, often glazed earthenware. Like the word "casserole," the name has also come to mean the food cooked in it. These days tians usually contain vegetables and herbs and sometimes cheese and eggs. This is a delicious version that can be served in spoonfuls or in wedges, with bread or a leafy side salad.

serves
4

Put the eggplant in a colander, sprinkle with the salt, and set aside for 15 minutes or until all the other ingredients have been prepared.

Preheat the oven to 400°F.

Heat the oil and 1 tablespoon of the butter in a large skillet, add the garlic, onion, scallions, spinach, and beans and sauté over medium heat for 6–8 minutes, stirring constantly, until the vegetables are soft but still colorful. Remove with a slotted spoon.

Pat the eggplant dry with paper towels, removing most of the salt. Add the remaining butter to the skillet, add the eggplant, and sauté for 5 minutes.

Put the eggs, crème fraîche, and Parmesan in a bowl and whisk with a fork.

Transfer the eggplant, vegetables, and their juices and oil into a shallow baking dish, distributing them evenly. Pour the egg and cheese mixture over the top and bake in the preheated oven for 5 minutes. Reduce the heat to 350°F for a further 20 minutes and cook until set and nicely browned.

1 small eggplant, cubed

2 teaspoons salt

2 tablespoons olive oil

2 tablespoons butter

4 garlic cloves, chopped

1 onion, sliced

4 scallions, sliced

a handful of spinach or Swiss chard, chopped

a handful of green beans, cut into 1-inch lengths

8 eggs

1 cup crème fraîche or sour cream

¾ cup grated Parmesan, Pecorino, or Gruyère

pumpkin and *gorgonzola* risotto

1 lb. pumpkin, peeled, seeded, and cubed

1 tablespoon olive oil

4 cups vegetable stock

2 tablespoons butter

1 leek, halved lengthwise and thinly sliced

1 garlic clove, chopped

1¾ cups risotto rice

2 oz. Gorgonzola, crumbled

 serves 4

This is similar to the Roasted Butternut Squash Risotto on page 135, but richer and altogether more special with the addition of luxuriously creamy Gorgonzola. It's also better for guests because the recipe serves 4 rather than 2. Make this in the fall when pumpkins are in season.

Preheat the oven to 350°F.

Put the pumpkin in a roasting pan, drizzle with the olive oil, and roast in the preheated oven for 30 minutes.

While the pumpkin is cooking in the oven, make the risotto. Put the stock in a saucepan. Heat until almost boiling, then reduce the heat until barely simmering to keep it hot.

Melt the butter in a large saucepan over high heat and add the leek and garlic. Cook for 4–5 minutes, stirring often, until the leeks have just softened.

Add the rice to the leeks and stir for 1 minute, until the rice is well coated with oil. Add a ladle of the hot stock to the rice and cook, stirring constantly, until the rice has absorbed most of the liquid. Repeat this process until all the liquid has been absorbed and the rice is tender but still firm (al dente), about 20–25 minutes.

Add the roasted pumpkin pieces. Remove the pan from the heat, stir in the Gorgonzola, and serve immediately.

fennel and *lemon* risotto

Fennel is a bit of an acquired taste, since it has a distinctive, aniseed-like flavor that's not to everyone's liking. If you do like it, and your friends are just as willing to eat it, make this light, basic risotto that will have everyone asking for more.

serves
4

2 fennel bulbs

4 cups vegetable stock

4 tablespoons unsalted butter

1 tablespoon olive oil

8 shallots, finely chopped

grated peel of 2 lemons

1½ cups risotto rice

½ cup white wine

1½ cups grated Parmesan

2 tablespoons light cream

salt and black pepper

Cut about ¼ inch from the gnarly stem on the bottom of the fennel bulbs. Cut off the fronds (the feathery leaves) and reserve. Cut off and discard all but about ½ inch from the dark green stems. Thinly slice the remaining white fennel bulb.

Put the stock in a saucepan. Heat until almost boiling, then reduce the heat until barely simmering to keep it hot.

Heat the butter and oil in a large saucepan over medium heat. Add the shallots and cook for 1–2 minutes, until softened but not browned. Add the fennel and lemon peel.

Add the rice and stir until the grains are well coated and glistening, about 1 minute. Pour in the wine and stir until it has been completely absorbed.

Add 1 ladle of hot stock and simmer, stirring until it has been absorbed. Continue to add the stock at intervals and cook as before, until the liquid has been absorbed and the rice is tender but still firm (al dente), about 18–20 minutes. Reserve the last ladle of stock.

Add the reserved stock, Parmesan, cream, and some salt and pepper. Mix well. Remove from the heat, cover, and let rest for 2 minutes. Spoon into bowls, top with the reserved fennel fronds, and serve.

risotto with *eggplant, pine nuts,* and *tomatoes*

serves
4

There are several steps to this risotto, but they all help to make the finished dish extra delicious. Salting the eggplant before cooking will remove any bitterness and toasting the pine nuts until golden will intensify their nutty flavor. This is really a complete entrée in one, with vegetables thrown in, so you probably won't need anything on the side.

1 small eggplant, about 7 oz., diced

⅛ cup pine nuts

3 tablespoons olive oil

4–6 firm tomatoes, seeded and chopped

4 cups vegetable stock

4 tablespoons unsalted butter

8 shallots, finely chopped

2 garlic cloves, crushed

1½ cups risotto rice

½ cup white wine

1½ cups grated Parmesan

a handful of parsley, freshly chopped

a handful of basil, freshly chopped

salt and black pepper

Put the eggplant in a colander set over a bowl. Sprinkle with salt and let stand for 10–15 minutes.

Meanwhile, heat a skillet over medium heat and drop in the pine nuts. Toast them, stirring frequently, until golden. Watch them carefully as they burn easily.

Rinse the eggplant to remove the salt and pat dry with paper towels. Heat 2 tablespoons of the oil in a skillet, add the eggplant, and cook until golden. Add the tomatoes and cook until softened.

Put the stock in a saucepan. Heat until almost boiling, then reduce the heat until barely simmering to keep it hot.

Heat the butter and remaining oil in a large saucepan over medium heat. Add the shallots and cook for 1–2 minutes, until softened but not browned. Add the garlic.

Add the rice and stir until the grains are well coated and glistening, about 1 minute. Pour in the wine and stir until it has been completely absorbed.

Add 1 ladle of hot stock and simmer, stirring until it has been absorbed. Continue to add the stock at intervals and cook as before, until the liquid has been absorbed and the rice is tender but firm (al dente), about 18–20 minutes. Reserve the last ladle of stock.

Add the reserved stock, the eggplant and tomato mixture, the Parmesan, pine nuts, parsley, basil, and some salt and pepper. Mix well. Remove from the heat, cover, and let rest for 2 minutes before serving.

*eggplant and
tomato stacks*

eggplant and tomato stacks

This is a smart and filling dish, with bubbly, molten cheese. Taleggio cheese is full of nuttiness when melted, but you could also use Gruyère or mozzarella. Beefsteak tomatoes are perfect here as they are large, great to slice, and easy to stack.

serves
4

1 eggplant, about 8 oz., sliced into 12 thick rounds

1 large beefsteak tomato, about 4 oz., sliced into 8 rounds

8 oz. Taleggio, or any other good melting cheese, cut into 8 slices

olive oil, for sprinkling

hot red pepper flakes, for sprinkling (optional)

Preheat the oven to 375°F.

Lightly brush a skillet with oil. Working in batches, add the eggplant slices and cook for a few minutes on each side until browned and softening.

To make the stacks, arrange 4 slices of eggplant apart in an oiled baking dish. Add 1 slice of tomato to each one, then 1 slice of cheese. Repeat until each stack has 3 slices of eggplant, 2 of tomato, and 3 of cheese, ending with eggplant. Sprinkle each stack with olive oil and pepper flakes, if using.

Bake in the preheated oven for about 15 minutes until soft, bubbly, and golden. Serve hot with a crisp green salad or lightly steamed vegetables.

pumpkin and feta packages

These are based on Argentinian empañadas, which are often filled with spiced meat, but this is a great vegetarian version.

makes
12

1 lb. pumpkin, peeled, seeded, and chopped

1 red onion, chopped

2 garlic cloves, crushed

½ teaspoon cumin seeds

2 tablespoons olive oil

2 teaspoons white wine vinegar

3 sheets of ready-rolled puff pastry, defrosted if frozen

3 oz. feta, grated

1 tablespoon milk

a baking sheet, lined with baking parchment

a cookie cutter, about 5 inches in diameter

Preheat the oven to 425°F.

Combine the pumpkin, onion, garlic, cumin, and oil in a small baking dish. Add the vinegar and ¼ cup water and cook in the oven for about 30 minutes, until the pumpkin is tender and golden and the liquid has evaporated. Transfer to a bowl (and leave the oven on), roughly mash with a fork, and season to taste. Set aside to cool.

Unroll the pastry and lay it on a clean work surface. Use the cookie cutter to stamp out 12 circles. Put 1 tablespoon of filling in the center of each circle and top with a little crumbled feta. Brush cold water around the edge of each one just to moisten and fold over to form a half-moon shape. Pinch the edges between your thumb and index finger to seal. Put on the prepared baking sheet. Brush the top of each with milk. Bake in the preheated oven for about 20 minutes, until lightly golden. Serve warm.

zucchini fritters

makes **15**

3 tablespoons olive oil, plus extra for frying

1 large onion, finely chopped

4 scallions, including green parts, chopped

2 garlic cloves, crushed

1¼ lbs. zucchini, trimmed and rinsed

2 small eggs

2 cups bread crumbs

4 tablespoons self-rising flour, plus 5–6 tablespoons, for rolling

6½ oz. feta, crumbled

1 cup grated Parmesan, Gruyère, or cheddar

1 tablespoon dried oregano

1 tablespoon dried mint

black pepper

If you've never made fritters before, try these! They are a popular snack in homes and restaurants of the Greek island called Alonnisos. The recipe makes about 15 so it's a great one to turn to when you're feeding a few people. Serve them with a tomato and arugula salad.

Heat the olive oil in a skillet, add the onion and scallions, and sauté gently until translucent, up to 20 minutes. Add the garlic, fry for 1 minute and remove from the heat. Let cool a little.

Grate the zucchini coarsely, put in a colander, and set aside for about 30 minutes to allow the excess moisture to seep out.

Put the eggs in a bowl and beat lightly. Squeeze the zucchini with your hands to extract as much moisture as possible—this is very important! Add to the bowl, then add the onion mixture, bread crumbs, the 4 tablespoons flour, feta, Parmesan, oregano, mint, and pepper. Mix with a fork. It should be dry enough to handle but, if not, add a little more flour.

Put a double sheet of baking parchment on a work surface and add the remaining flour. Take 1 tablespoon of the mixture, roll it in the flour, then make a round, flat shape with your hands, about 2 inches in diameter. The rounds are easier to handle when well coated in flour. Continue until the mixture is finished.

Heat some oil in a large, nonstick skillet and fry the fritters, in batches, for about 3 minutes on each side until crisp and golden. Drain on paper towels before serving.

*mushroom and
bell pepper tortilla*

mushroom and *bell pepper* tortilla

This tortilla is designed to be served as tapas—a traditional Spanish snack—and it's made particularly easy here because it is cooked in the oven. If you want to make the tapas in advance, serve them cold or reheat for a few minutes in a medium oven.

serves
4

3 tablespoons olive or safflower oil

2 potatoes, about 8 oz., peeled and thinly sliced

1 small onion, halved and thinly sliced

3 oz. button mushrooms, sliced

1 orange bell pepper, seeded and cut into strips

5 large eggs

1 teaspoon dried oregano

salt and black pepper

an 8-inch shallow, nonstick cake pan

Preheat the oven to 400°F.

Pour 1 tablespoon of the oil into the cake pan and put in the preheated oven to heat.

Meanwhile, heat the remaining oil in a large skillet, add the sliced potatoes and onion, and cook over medium heat for about 15 minutes, turning occasionally, until almost tender. Add the mushrooms and bell pepper and cook for 5 minutes.

Break the eggs into a large bowl and whisk briefly with a fork. Add the oregano and season with salt and pepper. Remove the vegetables from the pan with a slotted spoon, add to the bowl of eggs, and stir gently.

Transfer to the preheated cake pan, return to the oven, and cook for about 15–20 minutes, or until the egg is just set in the center. Let stand for about 10 minutes, then serve warm, cut into small squares.

grilled *bell pepper* frittata

1 small red bell pepper, quartered and seeded

1 small yellow bell pepper, quartered and seeded

1 small green bell pepper, quartered and seeded

2 tablespoons ricotta or mascarpone

6 large eggs

2 tablespoons freshly chopped thyme

2 tablespoons olive or safflower oil

1 large red onion, sliced

1 tablespoon balsamic vinegar

2 garlic cloves, crushed

salt and black pepper

This is colorful, packed with bell peppers, and perfect for preparing in advance. You can grill and peel the peppers the day before, if you like, then make the frittata itself on the morning that you're entertaining. It's delicious served hot or at room temperature. You can cut it into wedges or bars to serve as an appetizer, or if you're having a party, just double or triple the recipe, as necessary. The frittata is finished under the broiler so use a skillet with a heatproof handle.

Preheat the broiler to hot.

Put the bell peppers, skin-side up, under the broiler and cook until the skins have blackened. Transfer to a bowl, cover with a plate or plastic wrap, and let cool. This will steam off the skins, making them easier to remove.

Put the ricotta or mascarpone in a large bowl, add 1 egg, and mix to loosen the cheese. Whisk in the remaining eggs with a fork. Season with salt, pepper, and thyme and stir into the cheese mixture.

Peel the blackened skins off the peppers and rinse under cold running water. Pat dry with paper towels and cut into thick strips. Stir into the bowl.

Heat half the oil in a small skillet, add the sliced onion and balsamic vinegar, and cook over gentle heat for about 10 minutes until softened. Add the garlic and cook for 1 minute.

Using a slotted spoon, add the onion to the egg mixture and stir. Add the remaining oil to the skillet and heat gently. Pour the frittata mixture into the skillet and cook over low heat until almost set, puffy, and light golden brown on the underside.

Finish under a preheated broiler or put a plate or flat saucepan lid on top of the skillet and invert the skillet so the frittata drops onto the plate or lid. Slide back into the skillet and cook for 30–60 seconds. Transfer to a plate and serve hot or at room temperature, cut into wedges or bars.

asparagus, corn, and *goat cheese* frittata

Crunchy asparagus and corn work nicely here combined with eggs, creamy goat cheese, and fresh, tangy dill. You might think it's odd or annoying to use fresh corn ears for a frittata, but hopefully you will notice how much fresher and nicer it tastes than the frozen or canned variety. Plus, of course, your guests will appreciate the extra effort! That said, if you need to save time or you can't find fresh corn, use 8 oz. canned or frozen (and thawed) corn kernels instead. The frittata is finished under the broiler so use a skillet with a heatproof handle.

serves
4

2 bunches of thin asparagus spears

2 fresh ears of corn

3 tablespoons butter

4 scallions, finely chopped

a handful of dill, freshly chopped

8 eggs, beaten

7 oz. firm goat cheese, broken into pieces

salt and black pepper

Trim or snap off the woody ends from the asparagus and cut the spears into 1-inch pieces. Shuck the corn kernels from the ears of corn by very carefully holding one of the ears upright and slicing off the corn by running a knife downward. Mind your fingers!

Heat half of the butter in a large, nonstick skillet over medium heat. Add the asparagus, corn, and scallions and fry for 2–3 minutes, stirring often. Transfer the vegetables to a large bowl and add the dill, reserving a little to use as garnish. Wipe the skillet clean. Add the beaten eggs to the vegetables, gently stirring to combine, and season with salt and pepper.

Preheat the broiler to high.

Put the remaining butter in the skillet and set over high heat. Swirl the skillet around as the butter melts so that it coats the bottom and just starts to sizzle. Pour the frittata mixture into the skillet and reduce the heat to medium. Arrange the pieces of goat cheese over the top of the frittata and gently push them into the mixture. Cook for about 8 minutes, until the sides of the frittata start to puff up (reduce the heat if the bottom appears to be cooking too quickly).

Keep the frittata in the skillet and place it under the preheated broiler. Cook for 1 minute only just to set the top. Let cool a little in the skillet, sprinkle with the reserved dill, and serve immediately.

soufflé cheese omelet

soufflé *cheese* omelet

4 large eggs, separated

2 tomatoes, halved horizontally

a small pat of butter

⅓ cup grated cheddar

salt and black pepper

serves
2

Q

This is the breakfast or brunch you want to make for a special someone. It's a soufflé-like omelet that's easy to whip up but looks like you've made a real effort. Serve it with the broiled tomato and some toast on the side and you're guaranteed to be in the good books. Don't forget to make some for yourself too!

Preheat the broiler to medium. Line the broiler pan with foil.

Meanwhile, whisk the egg whites in a large, clean bowl until they form stiff peaks. It will be much quicker if you do this with a handheld electric whisk. Season the egg yolks with salt and pepper and beat them in a separate bowl until even in color and texture. Carefully fold the egg whites into the egg yolks using a metal spoon.

Put the tomatoes under the broiler and cook for 6–8 minutes, turning once. After the tomato has been cooking for 4 minutes, heat the butter in a medium-sized nonstick skillet. When the butter has melted, swirl it around the skillet to cover the base.

Tip the egg mixture into the skillet and flatten gently with a spatula until it covers the base of the skillet. Cook over medium heat for 2 minutes, then sprinkle the cheese over the center of the omelet. Cook for another minute, or until the base is light golden.

Carefully fold the omelet in half to cover the cheese. When the egg is set, slide onto a plate. Serve with the broiled tomato and some toast.

squash and *sage* frittata

There is something about the musty sharpness of sage that works so well with the sweetness of caramelized squash. Like other frittatas and tortillas, this is a very adaptable dish—cut into wedges and served with a green salad, it makes a great lunch. Cut into much smaller, bite-size pieces, it works well as a nibble for a drinks party. Stuffed into a hollowed-out crusty loaf and drizzled with olive oil, it's even suitable for a picnic! The frittata is finished under the broiler so use a skillet with a heatproof handle (and a lid, for the first step).

serves
4

¼ cup olive oil

2 large onions, halved and thinly sliced

¼ teaspoon hot red pepper flakes (or more to taste)

2 garlic cloves, halved

1 butternut squash (about 1¼ lbs.), peeled, seeded, and cut into 1-inch dice

1 tablespoon freshly chopped sage

8 large eggs

2–3 tablespoons freshly chopped parsley

1 tablespoon butter

4 oz. firm goat cheese, cubed

salt and black pepper

Heat the oil in a large skillet over medium heat. Add the onions and 2 good pinches of salt. Stir, then cover and reduce the heat to low. Cook very gently, stirring occasionally, until the onions are meltingly soft and golden yellow, about 20 minutes.

Raise the heat slightly and add the pepper flakes, garlic, and squash. Stir well. Cook gently, stirring frequently, until the squash is just tender, about 10 minutes. Discard the garlic. Fry the squash a little more until it starts to brown, then stir in the sage and cook for a few more minutes. Let it cool slightly.

Preheat the broiler to medium.

In a bowl, whisk the eggs and beat in the parsley, then stir in the cooked squash and onions. Season with a little salt and black pepper.

Put the skillet back over medium heat. Add the butter to the skillet, and as it foams, pour in the egg and squash mixture and use a spatula to level it. Scatter the goat cheese evenly over the top. Cook for about 5–6 minutes until the underside is golden brown and set. Put the frittata under the broiler and cook until it is evenly browned, slightly puffed up, and the egg is fully set. Serve warm or at room temperature.

roast *tomato, goat cheese,* and *arugula* tartlets

Ingredients

2 x 12-oz. packages of ready-rolled puff pastry, defrosted if frozen

2 tablespoons olive oil

2 tablespoons tomato paste

a handful of basil, freshly chopped

6 ripe tomatoes

3½ oz. firm goat cheese, crumbled

1 teaspoon sugar

a handful of arugula or watercress

1 oz. Parmesan, shaved with a vegetable peeler

salt and black pepper

flour, for dusting

serves 4

Your guests will be delighted with these homemade tartlets. There's something about individual little tarts that looks so impressive and professional. The pastry can be cooked ahead of time and the topping added at the last moment. Ready-rolled puff pastry is a great help for cooks with little time to spare.

Preheat the oven to 425°F.

Lightly flour a work surface. Lay out the pastry and cut it into 4 x 6-inch rounds using a small plate as a guide. Prick all over vigorously with a fork and place on a baking sheet. Cover with baking parchment, then put another baking sheet on top. Bake in the preheated oven for 15–20 minutes until golden brown. Cooking the pastry this way will ensure that it does not puff up too much but remains crisp. Remove from the oven and set aside.

Preheat the broiler to high.

Mix together the olive oil, tomato paste, and chopped basil. Spread this mixture over the cooked pastry rounds right to the edge.

If you have time, skin the tomatoes. To do this, follow the instructions under Ingredients Tips on page 10.

Slice the tomatoes finely and arrange them on top of the cooked pastry rounds, making sure they overlap and reach the edges, otherwise the pastry edges will burn. Scatter the goat cheese over the top, season with salt and pepper, and sprinkle over the sugar.

Put the tarts on a baking sheet and place under the broiler to cook until the cheese begins to melt and bubble. Transfer to plates and top each tart with arugula or watercress and Parmesan shavings. Serve immediately.

Variation You can use other cheeses, such as crumbled feta, sliced mozzarella, cubed Roquefort, or grated cheddar.

upside-down *tomato* tart

This is a version of a tarte Tatin, a French tart essentially made upside-down on the stove to start with, then baked in the oven. The good news is that you need barely any ingredients, and you buy the pastry ready-made and ready-rolled so there's very little for you to do! This tart combines fresh rosemary and little capers but you could add any combination of ingredients that takes your fancy, such as olives, oregano, or garlic. It serves 4 as an appetizer or 2 as a generous entrée. This tart is finished in the oven so use a skillet with a heatproof handle.

Preheat the oven to 425°F.

Put the oil, capers, and rosemary in a medium, nonstick skillet. Put over high heat and when the capers start to sizzle add the tomatoes, firmly pressing them down in a single layer in the skillet. Cook for 3–4 minutes to allow the tomatoes to sizzle and soften.

Place the sheet of pastry over the tomatoes, folding in the corners and being careful not to press down on the tomatoes. Transfer the skillet to the preheated oven and cook for 18–20 minutes, until the pastry is puffed and golden. Remove the skillet from the oven and let the tart rest for a couple of minutes.

Place a serving plate that is larger than the skillet upside-down on top of the skillet and quickly flip the skillet over so the tart falls onto the plate. Sprinkle with black pepper and a drizzle of olive oil and cut into wedges.

serves
2–4

2 tablespoons olive oil, plus extra for drizzling

2 teaspoons capers, rinsed if salted

10–12 fresh rosemary needles

3 ripe tomatoes, thickly sliced

12-oz. package of ready-rolled puff pastry, defrosted if frozen

black pepper

tomato and *olive* tart with *parmesan*

12-oz. packet of ready-rolled puff pastry, defrosted if frozen

4 oz. red cherry tomatoes, halved

4 oz. yellow cherry tomatoes, halved

½ cup semi-dried or sun-dried tomatoes, halved

½ cup pitted black olives, halved

2 tablespoons olive oil

1 oz. Parmesan, shaved with a vegetable peeler

salt and black pepper

flour, for dusting

a handful of arugula, to serve

The loveliest thing about this tart is its vibrant colors, so try to find yellow cherry tomatoes to complement the regular red ones. If you are lucky enough to have a market near you, you might find them there. Serve simply with arugula.

Preheat the oven to 425°F.

Lightly flour a baking sheet. Lay out the pastry and roll it or cut it as necessary to form a rectangle, about 10 x 12 inches. Using the blade of a sharp knife, gently tap the edges several times (this will help the pastry rise and the edges separate) and prick all over with a fork.

Put the tomatoes, olives, oil, and some salt and pepper in a bowl and mix lightly. Spoon the mixture over the pastry. Bake in the preheated oven for about 12–15 minutes until risen and golden.

Remove from the oven and sprinkle with the Parmesan. Cut into 3 or 4 slices and serve hot with a handful of arugula.

belgian *leek* tart

This tart is a little like a quiche—but for cheats! Use a storebought pastry case and all you have to do is make the filling. There is nothing quite like the combination of meltingly soft sweet leeks, cream, and pastry.

serves
4–6

5 tablespoons butter

2 lbs. leeks, thickly sliced

1 teaspoon salt

4 egg yolks

1¼ cups heavy cream or crème fraîche

grated nutmeg, to taste

a ready-made 8-inch shortcrust pastry case

salt and black pepper

Preheat the oven to 400°F.

Melt the butter in a large saucepan and add the leeks, stirring to coat. Add a few tablespoons of water and the 1 teaspoon salt, and cover with a lid. Steam very gently for at least 30 minutes (trying not to look too often!) until soft and melting. Remove the lid and cook for a few minutes to evaporate any excess liquid—the mixture should be quite thick. Let cool.

Put the egg yolks and cream or crème fraîche into a bowl, add salt, pepper, and nutmeg to taste, and beat well. Set the ready-made pastry case on a baking sheet. Spoon the cooled leeks evenly into the pastry case, fluffing them up a bit with a fork. Pour the eggs and cream mixture over the top.

Bake in the preheated oven for 30 minutes or until set and pale golden brown. Serve warm.

desserts

juicy fruit crisp

juicy *fruit* crisp

Lovely at any time of year, this dessert is a combination of juicy fruits and a crunchy topping. Eat warm or cold with ice cream or yogurt.

serves
4

2 large Granny Smith apples or 2 medium pears, peeled, cored, and chopped

1¾ cups fresh or frozen raspberries, blueberries, or blackberries (no need to thaw)

2 tablespoons white or brown sugar

Topping

1 cup all-purpose flour

⅛ cup brown sugar

6 tablespoons unsalted butter, chilled and cubed

a medium baking dish, greased

Preheat the oven to 375°F.

Put the fruit in the dish, then add the berries. Sprinkle with the sugar and toss gently until just mixed. Spread the fruit evenly in the dish.

To make the topping, put the flour, sugar, and butter in a mixing bowl. Using your fingertips, rub the mixture together until it becomes soft and sticky and there are pea-size lumps of dough. Sprinkle this mixture over the fruit but don't press it down.

Bake in the preheated oven for 25 minutes until bubbling and golden on top. Serve the crisp hot, warm, or cold.

pan *plum* crumble

This comforting crumble is cooked under the broiler and you can even serve it at the table straight out of the skillet—it doesn't get any more casual than that! The crumble is finished under the broiler so use a skillet with a heatproof handle.

serves
4–6

Q

¾ cup orange juice

2 tablespoons white sugar

6 ripe plums, halved and pitted

¾ cup self-rising flour

⅛ cup packed brown sugar

½ cup rolled oats

4 tablespoons unsalted butter, chilled and cubed

Put the orange juice and white sugar in a small skillet over high heat. Bring the mixture to a boil, then reduce the heat to medium. Add the plums, cut-side down, and cook for 5 minutes. Turn the plums over and cook for a further 5 minutes, until they have softened yet still retain their shape and the liquid has almost evaporated. Remove the skillet from the heat and set aside.

Preheat the broiler to medium.

Put the flour, brown sugar, and oats in a bowl and mix just to combine. Add the butter and use your fingertips to rub it into the dry ingredients.

Sprinkle the mixture evenly over the plums and slide the skillet under the broiler for 2–3 minutes, until the crumble is golden. Serve warm.

nectarine and pistachio crumble

Crumbles are normally considered to be a comforting winter dessert, but this deliciously light, nutty version makes the most of juicy summer nectarines. It takes very little time to prepare and, like most crumbles, tastes sublime with ice cream.

½ cup shelled pistachio nuts, finely chopped

⅛ cup ground almonds

½ cup ground oatmeal or oat flour

4 tablespoons unsalted butter, chilled and cubed

½ cup all-purpose flour

¼ cup packed brown sugar

6 nectarines

Preheat the oven to 425°F.

Put the pistachio nuts, almonds, oatmeal, and butter in a mixing bowl. Use your fingertips to rub the ingredients together until the mixture resembles coarse bread crumbs. Add the flour and sugar and rub together to combine. At this stage, you can cover and refrigerate the topping until needed.

Line a baking sheet with baking parchment. Cut the nectarines in half. If the pit does not come out easily, don't worry—simply slice the flesh off the fruit and drop it directly onto the baking sheet. Sprinkle the crumble topping evenly over the nectarines and bake in the preheated oven for about 10–15 minutes, until the fruit is soft and juicy and the topping is a golden color. Serve warm.

double chocolate fruity squares

This is great! It's similar to refrigerator cake (so it doesn't need baking) but made with dried fruit, and margarine instead of butter, so it's a healthy option.

6½ oz. semisweet chocolate

7 tablespoons sunflower margarine

2 tablespoons orange juice

4 oz. graham crackers

2 oz. white chocolate

¼ cup raisins

⅛ cup dried apricots, chopped

¼ cup dried cherries or cranberries

a baking pan, 8 inches square, lightly greased

Break the semisweet chocolate into small squares and put them in a saucepan. Add the margarine and orange juice and heat very gently for 3–4 minutes, stirring occasionally, until melted. Stir until smooth.

Put the graham crackers in a polythene bag and crush with a rolling pin. Roughly chop the white chocolate. Add the crushed crackers, white chocolate, and all the dried fruit to the melted chocolate mixture. Stir well.

Spoon the mixture into the prepared baking pan and press down lightly with the back of a wooden spoon. Transfer to the refrigerator and let set for at least 2 hours. Cut into squares to serve. Store lightly covered in the refrigerator for up to 4 days.

nectarine and
pistachio crumble

coconut creamed rice with poached plums

Canned coconut milk is a useful ingredient to have in your kitchen, as it can be used in lots of dishes, both savory and sweet. When you're buying the plums for this recipe, choose a sweet, large variety of plum and pick fruits with a silvery patina, as it's an indicator of freshness. The coconut creamed rice is also lovely with poached cherries.

serves
6

8 plums, halved and pitted

½ cup raw sugar

1 cinnamon stick

2 cardamom pods

Coconut creamed rice

¼ cup short grain rice

2 x 14-oz. cans coconut milk

¼ cup sugar

½ cup whipping cream

To make the coconut creamed rice, put the rice in a strainer and rinse it under cold running water until the water runs clear. Drain well. Put the rice in a large saucepan over high heat and add the coconut milk and sugar. Bring to a gentle boil, then reduce the heat to low and cook for about 25–30 minutes, stirring often to ensure that the rice doesn't catch. Let cool. Whip the cream until soft peaks form, then fold it into the rice mixture.

Meanwhile, put the plums, sugar, cinnamon stick, and cardamom pods in a saucepan and add 1 cup water. Bring to a boil, then reduce the heat to low and cook for 20 minutes, gently turning the plums often, until they soften but retain their shape. Remove the cinnamon stick and cardamom pods from the pan.

Divide the creamed rice between dishes and spoon the warm plums over the top. Serve immediately.

raspberry and *almond* tart

serves
6–8

This tart tastes better the day after it's made, which makes it ideal for preparing ahead of time. Be aware that you will need to freeze the raspberries before you start baking. This makes them firm enough to retain their shape while they're baking and stops them bleeding into the tart.

1 egg

3 tablespoons sugar

1 tablespoon all-purpose flour, plus extra for dusting

5 tablespoons unsalted butter

5 oz. raspberries, scattered on a tray and frozen until firm

chilled cream, to serve (optional)

Pastry

⅓ cup ground almonds

1¼ cups all-purpose flour

5 tablespoons sugar

1 stick unsalted butter, chilled and cubed

a rectangular tart pan, 5 x 8 inches, lightly greased

Preheat the oven to 350°F.

To make the pastry, put the ground almonds, flour, and sugar in a mixing bowl. Add the butter and mix in with your fingertips until the mixture resembles coarse bread crumbs. Add 2 tablespoons cold water and bring together until just combined.

Tip the pastry out onto a lightly floured work surface and knead to form a ball. Roll it out between 2 layers of baking parchment until it is about 2 inches longer and 2 inches wider than the tart pan. Carefully lift the pastry into the pan and use your fingers to press it down into the base and sides, letting it overhang. Prick the base all over with a fork and bake in the preheated oven for 20 minutes, until lightly golden. Break off the overhanging pastry. Leave the oven on.

Put the egg, sugar, and flour in a bowl and use a whisk to beat until thick and pale. Put the butter in a small saucepan over medium heat. Let melt until frothy and dark golden, with a nutty aroma. Working quickly, pour the melted butter over the egg mixture and beat well.

Scatter the frozen raspberries in the tart case. Pour the warm batter over the raspberries. Bake in the oven for about 45 minutes, until the top resembles a golden meringue. Let cool for 30 minutes before serving. Cut into slices and serve with chilled cream if you like.

chocolate and *hazelnut* brownies

3½ oz. semisweet chocolate, broken into pieces

2 tablespoons milk

1 stick sunflower margarine

1 cup raw sugar

2 eggs, beaten

⅓ cup unsweetened cocoa powder

½ cup self-rising flour

⅓ cup chopped hazelnuts

a baking pan, 8 inches square, lightly greased and lined with baking parchment

makes
9

Everyone loves chocolate brownies. These are a slightly healthier version because they use sunflower margarine instead of butter. They also include hazelnuts but you can of course use pecans or walnuts if you prefer. Serve the brownie squares as an afternoon treat, in a packed lunch, at parties or as a dessert with fresh raspberries.

Preheat the oven to 325°F.

Put the chocolate in a saucepan with the milk and heat gently, stirring, until the chocolate is melted and smooth. Remove the pan from the heat and let cool slightly.

Put the margarine and sugar in a large bowl and beat with a handheld electric whisk or a wooden spoon until the mixture is light and fluffy. Beat in the eggs a little at a time, beating well after each addition, until blended. Sift the cocoa powder into the egg mixture and stir gently until mixed. Pour in the melted chocolate and stir well.

Gently stir in the flour and hazelnuts—do not beat or overmix or the brownies will be dry. Spoon the mixture into the prepared pan and smooth the top. Bake in the preheated oven for about 25 minutes. To test if they are cooked, insert a skewer into the center; it should come out almost clean with a slightly sticky feel.

Remove the brownies from the oven and let cool before cutting into squares. Store in an airtight container for up to 1 week, or wrap and freeze for up to 1 month.

baked *apples* and *pears*

Baked fruit is both easy on the cook and easy on the waistline. This recipe gives quantities for two servings to make it simple to increase as needed. These are really good served with a dollop of plain, unsweetened Greek yogurt.

serves 2

Preheat the oven to 400°F.

Peel the apples. If necessary, trim the bottoms slightly so that they sit flat. Using a small knife or a corer, remove the cores. With a small spoon, scrape out some apple around the core cavity to allow for more stuffing. Peel the pear, halve, and scoop out the core, as for the apple.

In a small bowl, mix together the hazelnuts, raisins, and apricots.

Arrange the apples and pears in the baking dish. Stuff the nut mixture into the apple and pear cavities, mounding it on top. Top each with a light sprinkling of cinnamon and a good knob of butter, then drizzle each with 1–2 teaspoons of honey, to taste. Cover with foil.

Bake in the preheated oven for 20 minutes, then remove the foil and continue baking until just golden, about 10–15 minutes. Divide the apples and pears carefully between serving plates and pour over any pan juices. Serve warm with plain Greek yogurt if you like.

baked apples and pears

2 apples, preferably Cox's or Braeburn

1 just-ripe pear, preferably Conference

2 tablespoons chopped hazelnuts

1 tablespoon golden raisins

4–5 dried apricots, chopped

ground cinnamon, for dusting

2 tablespoons unsalted butter

honey, to drizzle

a nonstick baking dish, large enough to comfortably hold the fruit

summer *fruit* bars

These bars have a lovely fruity surprise sandwiched in the center—a juicy layer of summer berries. Serve them with an extra helping of berries. A scoop of vanilla ice cream is also delicious. If fresh berries are out of season, you can buy a bag of frozen fruit instead.

makes
16

2 cups all-purpose flour

1¼ cups ground almonds

1 stick plus 7 tablespoons unsalted butter, softened

1 cup sugar

2 eggs, lightly beaten

10 oz. mixed summer berries, such as raspberries, strawberries, and blackberries, plus extra to serve

an 8-inch square cake pan, greased and baselined with baking parchment

Preheat the oven to 350°F.

Put the flour, almonds, butter, sugar, and eggs in a mixing bowl and mix to a soft dough. Divide the mixture in half.

Press one half of the dough into the prepared pan. The easiest way to do this is to take a small handful of dough, flatten it slightly in your hand, then press it into the pan. Repeat to make an even layer about ½ inch thick.

Lightly press the summer berries into the dough in an even layer. Top the fruit with the remaining dough, covering it in an even layer using the method above.

Put the pan in the center of the preheated oven and bake for 35–40 minutes until the top is light golden. Remove from the oven and transfer to a wire rack to cool for 10 minutes.

To remove the cake from the pan, put the wire rack on top of the pan and carefully turn it over so the rack is on the bottom—the cake should slide out of the pan. Peel away the parchment lining, then turn the cake over. Cut into 16 bars and serve with berries.

rhubarb and custard pots

baked cheesecake

rhubarb and *custard* pots

serves
6

These are very pretty desserts, perfect for entertaining, as they can be made well in advance and popped in the fridge until you are ready to serve. Note that early forced rhubarb is more tender and will cook much more quickly than the later, ruby-colored stalks. Keep your eye on it as it cooks. You don't want a pink mush, but rather a softly poached fruit that's still intact.

1¼ lbs. rhubarb, trimmed and chopped into 1-inch pieces

3 tablespoons sugar

1 teaspoon grated orange peel

2 tablespoons orange juice

Custard

1 cup light cream

1 cup heavy cream

1 vanilla bean, split lengthwise by running a small, sharp knife down the bean

4 egg yolks

2 tablespoons sugar

2 tablespoons slivered almonds, toasted in a dry skillet

Put the rhubarb, sugar, orange peel and juice, and 2 tablespoons water in a saucepan over high heat. Cook, stirring constantly, until the mixture boils. Reduce the heat to medium and simmer for 5 minutes, until the rhubarb is soft but still retains some shape. Spoon the rhubarb into 6 individual serving dishes and set aside to cool while you make the custard.

Put both the light and heavy cream in a saucepan. Set over low heat and add the vanilla bean. Slowly bring the cream to a boil. As the cream boils, remove the bean and scrape the seeds into the custard, discarding the bean. Put the egg yolks and sugar in a bowl and whisk for 1 minute. Slowly pour the hot cream into the yolk mixture, whisking constantly. Transfer the mixture to a clean saucepan and set over low heat. Cook for 5 minutes, being careful not to let it boil until thickened.

While still warm, spoon the custard over the rhubarb and let the pots cool in the fridge for at least 3 hours or overnight before serving.

baked cheesecake

This is food to impress. Make it the day before you serve it and don't stress about cracks in the surface—they add character! For the best result, bring the cream cheese, eggs, and sour cream to room temperature before using.

serves 10

5 oz. very dry, slightly sweet cookies, such as tea biscuits or graham crackers

1 cup plus 2 tablespoons sugar

7 tablespoons unsalted butter, melted

1 lb. 10 oz. cream cheese

5 eggs

1 teaspoon grated lemon peel

1¼ cups sour cream

a springform cake pan, 9 inches in diameter, lined with baking parchment and lightly greased

Preheat the oven to 325°F. Wrap the entire outside of the prepared cake pan in 2 layers of foil.

Put the cookies in a polythene bag and crush with a rolling pin. Pour into a bowl with 1 tablespoon of the sugar. Add the melted butter and mix until well combined. Tip the crumb mixture into the prepared pan and spread evenly over the base. Use the bottom of a glass tumbler to firmly press the crumb mixture into the pan. Bake in the preheated oven for 20 minutes (and leave the oven on). Remove and let cool completely.

Put the cream cheese and remaining sugar in a bowl and beat for about 2 minutes, until smooth and well combined. Add the eggs, one at a time, beating well between each addition and scraping down the side of the bowl. Add the lemon peel and sour cream. Beat until lump-free.

Pour the mixture into the prepared pan and level the top with a knife. Bake in the oven for 1 hour, until the top is golden but the center is still wobbly. Turn the oven off and partially open the oven door. Let the cheesecake cool in the oven for 1 hour. Refrigerate for 6 hours, or ideally overnight.

Remove the cheesecake from the refrigerator 1 hour before eating. When ready to serve, run a warm, dry knife around the edge of the cake and remove the springform side. Cut into generous wedges.

coconut caramel sauce

Coconut milk adds an exotic twist to caramel sauce, which makes the perfect addition to the Pan-fried Caribbean Bananas on page 227 or to grilled mango.

serves 4

Q

½ cup packed brown sugar

7 tablespoons unsalted butter

¾ cup coconut milk

Heat all the ingredients in a small saucepan until the sugar dissolves. Bring to a boil and simmer for 8–10 minutes, or until the sauce is thick and glossy. Serve warm.

almond and lemon cake

almond and _lemon_ cake

Lemons and almonds are a flavor match made in heaven and they're divine here in this cake. It's the perfect no-fuss recipe for feeding a sweet-toothed crowd.

serves 10

Preheat the oven to 350°F.

Finely grate the peel from 2 of the lemons and squeeze all 3 of them so that you have ⅓ cup lemon juice. Put the butter, sugar, and lemon peel in a bowl and, using a handheld electric whisk or a wooden spoon, beat for about 5 minutes, until the mixture is thick. Add the eggs, 1 at a time, and beat well between each addition. Fold in the flour, baking powder, and ground almonds. Add the lemon juice and stir to combine. Spoon the mixture into the prepared pan and bake in the preheated oven for about 35 minutes, until the top of the cake is golden and the center springs back when gently pressed. Remove from the pan and let cool.

To make the lemon icing, beat the confectioners' sugar with the lemon juice for 2 minutes. Drizzle the icing over the cake and let set before serving.

3 lemons

1 stick plus 6 tablespoons unsalted butter

⅔ cup sugar

3 eggs

½ cup all-purpose flour

1 teaspoon baking powder

1⅔ cups ground almonds

Lemon icing

⅔ cup confectioners' sugar

2 tablespoons lemon juice

an 8-inch square cake pan, baselined with baking parchment and lightly greased

pan-fried caribbean _bananas_

This dessert is superb topped with a dollop of crème fraîche or sour cream, and perhaps a sprinkling of pumpkin seeds. It's super-quick, and quite healthy, so you don't need to feel guilty about having dessert after a big meal!

serves 2

Q

Melt the margarine and honey in a nonstick skillet over high heat. Add the bananas and fry for 2–3 minutes until they are golden and softened.

Quickly stir in the raisins, rum, if using, and orange juice. Bubble for about 30 seconds, then spoon into bowls and serve immediately.

1 tablespoon margarine

1 tablespoon honey

2 bananas, sliced

2 tablespoons golden raisins

1 tablespoon dark rum (optional)

juice of 1 small orange

2–3 tablespoons honey

1–2 teaspoons ground ginger

14 oz. rhubarb, trimmed and
chopped into 1-inch pieces

¾ cup sour cream or
crème fraîche

2 tablespoons confectioners'
sugar

1 tablespoon grated
lemon peel

ginger, rhubarb, and cream cups

 makes 4

The bite of the ginger and rhubarb against the mellowness of
the cream makes this dessert irresistible. Eat it straight from
a large bowl for a mid-week treat.

Put the honey, ground ginger, and ⅔ cup water in a skillet. Heat gently over
medium heat and slowly bring to a boil, stirring occasionally. Reduce the
heat and simmer for 10 minutes. Add the rhubarb to the skillet and simmer
for a further 8 minutes, until the rhubarb is soft but still retaining its shape.
Remove the skillet from the heat and let cool.

Drain the rhubarb, then divide it between 4 glasses. Refrigerate for 1 hour.
Just before serving, put the sour cream or crème fraîche, sugar, and lemon
peel in a bowl and mix. Spoon the mixture on top of the rhubarb.

strawberry tartlets

 serves 6

These basic little tarts are made of a rich shortbread topped
with small strawberries and a glossy, professional glaze.

1¾ cups all-purpose flour

½ cup confectioners' sugar

1½ sticks unsalted butter,
chilled and cubed

2 large egg yolks

½ teaspoon vanilla extract

a little butter, for greasing

Strawberry topping

about ⅔ cup raspberry jelly

about 1 lb. small
strawberries, hulled

2 baking sheets, greased

a pastry brush

Sift the flour and confectioners' sugar into a mixing bowl. Add the butter
and mix with your fingertips until it looks like fine bread crumbs. Add the
egg yolks and vanilla and mix until the dough comes together. Wrap the
dough in plastic wrap and refrigerate for 30 minutes.

Divide the dough into 6. Roll each piece into a ball and put on the prepared
baking sheets, setting them well apart. Press the dough to make circles
about ¼ inch thick. Pinch the edges with your fingers, then prick the bases
all over with a fork. Refrigerate for 10 minutes.

Meanwhile, preheat the oven to 350°F.

Bake the circles in the preheated oven for 20 minutes until they are a light
golden color. Let cool on the sheets.

To make the strawberry topping, put the jelly in a small saucepan with
1 tablespoon water and heat gently. Remove from the heat before it starts
to boil. Set each cooked pastry circle on a plate. Using a pastry brush, brush
a little hot jelly over each circle. Arrange the strawberries on the base and
brush with the hot glaze. Let set—about 20 minutes—before serving.

strawberry tartlets

berries with honeyed yogurt

berries with *honeyed yogurt*

Dessert doesn't get simpler than this. When you just have to satisfy a sweet, after-dinner craving but you don't want a full-blown sweet treat, try this. It's refreshing and delicious.

Reserve a few of the best berries for serving and put the remainder into a saucepan. Add the lemon peel, lemon juice, cinnamon, and 1 tablespoon water. Heat gently for about 3 minutes until the berries just start to soften slightly. Let cool.

Spoon the berries into 4–6 glasses, then add the yogurt and honey. Top with the reserved berries and serve.

serves
4–6

Q

7 oz. blueberries

a strip of lemon peel

a squeeze of lemon juice

a pinch of ground cinnamon

2¾ cups plain yogurt

⅓ cup honey

strawberry sundaes

serves 2

Q

9 oz. very ripe strawberries, hulled

1 cup vanilla yogurt

¾ cup Greek yogurt

½ cup teaspoon vanilla extract (optional)

6 amaretti cookies, roughly broken

Layers of fresh strawberry sauce and crushed amaretti cookies are interspersed with creamy vanilla yogurt custard to make a delicious dessert.

Set aside 4 strawberries to decorate. Purée the remaining fruit by pressing it through a strainer. Set aside.

Mix together the vanilla yogurt, Greek yogurt, and vanilla extract, if using, in a bowl.

Spoon a layer of the yogurt mixture into 2 tall glasses. Top with a layer of strawberry purée and amaretti cookies. Repeat with another layer of yogurt mixture, the remaining purée and amaretti. Top with a final layer of yogurt mixture.

Slice the reserved strawberries and use to decorate the sundaes.

melon with ginger syrup

serves 4–6

Q

4 tablespoons sugar

1 inch fresh ginger, peeled and finely chopped

juice of ½ large lemon

1 large, ripe melon

Melon and ginger are a classic combination of flavors and this simple version is perfect for a warm summer's day. You can use any type of melon, but cantaloupe works particularly well.

Put the sugar and ⅔ cup water into a small saucepan and heat gently to dissolve the sugar. Bring to a boil, add the ginger and lemon juice, and simmer gently for 3 minutes. Remove from the heat and let cool.

Cut the melon into wedges, scoop out the seeds, and serve drizzled with ginger syrup.

strawberry sundaes

triple *chocolate* pancakes

Complete chocolate overload! These wicked little pancakes are packed with velvety melted chocolate and finished with the sweet and sour taste of smooth white chocolate yogurt.

makes 12

Sift the flour, cocoa, baking powder, baking soda, and sugar into a bowl. Put the milk, buttermilk, egg yolks, and cooled melted butter into a second large bowl and beat well. Add the flour mixture and mix thoroughly.

Put the egg whites and salt into a clean bowl and whisk with a handheld electric whisk until stiff peaks form. Add 1 tablespoon of the egg whites to the chocolate mixture and stir to loosen it, then carefully fold in the remaining egg whites, then the bittersweet and white chocolate.

Heat a greased skillet over medium heat. Reduce the heat. Pour about 2 tablespoons of batter into the skillet and cook in batches of 3–4 over low heat for about 1 minute, or until small bubbles begin to appear on the surface and the underside is golden brown. Turn the pancakes over and cook the other side for 1 minute. Transfer to a plate and keep them warm in a low oven while you cook the remainder.

To make the white chocolate yogurt, put the chocolate into a bowl set over a saucepan of simmering water and melt slowly. Do not let the base of the bowl touch the water. Remove from the heat and let cool a little, then beat in the yogurt until smooth and shiny. Serve with the pancakes and Hot Chocolate Sauce.

1½ cups all-purpose flour

¾ cup unsweetened cocoa powder

1 teaspoon baking powder

1 teaspoon baking soda

¼ cup sugar

¾ cup milk

½ cup buttermilk

2 eggs, separated

2 tablespoons unsalted butter, melted and cooled

½ teaspoon salt

3 oz. bittersweet chocolate, chopped

3 oz. white chocolate, chopped

Hot Chocolate Sauce (page 234), to serve

White chocolate yogurt

6 oz. white chocolate, broken into pieces

¼ cup plain yogurt

scotch pancakes

makes
12

Q

¾ cup self-rising flour

a pinch of salt

1 egg

2 tablespoons superfine sugar, plus extra to serve

½ cup milk

3 tablespoons unsalted butter, plus extra to serve

Scotch pancakes should be served warm, more or less straight from the skillet, spread with butter and sprinkled with sugar.

Put the flour and salt in a large mixing bowl, make a dip in the center, and add the egg, sugar, and milk. Melt 2 tablespoons of the butter in a small saucepan, then add to the mixing bowl. Work the mixture together with a whisk or wooden spoon to make a smooth batter. Beat for 1 minute, then set aside for 10 minutes.

Set a skillet over medium heat, add the remaining butter, and when it melts, swish it around the skillet, then pour off the excess into a small heatproof bowl. Put the skillet back on the heat and spoon 1 tablespoon of the batter into the skillet. Cook until the pancake browns and bubbles appear on the surface, then turn it over. Transfer to a plate and keep it warm in a low oven while you cook the remainder. Return a little of the melted butter back to the skillet as necessary. Serve immediately, spread with butter and sprinkled with sugar.

chocolate-dipped *fruit*

serves
4

1 lb. fresh, ripe, but firm fruit, such as strawberries, apples, seedless grapes, or satsumas

Hot chocolate sauce

3½ oz. semisweet chocolate, broken into pieces

1 teaspoon corn syrup

a few toothpicks or skewers

This is fun food—not very sophisticated (unless you stick to strawberries and dip them neatly into the chocolate) but all the better for it. There's something pleasing about healthy fruit smothered in irresistible melted chocolate.

Wash the fruit and dry it carefully with paper towels. Leave the small fruit whole. Cut the apples into thin wedges and remove the core. Divide the satsumas into segments.

Put the chocolate and corn syrup into a bowl set over a saucepan of simmering water and melt slowly. Do not let the base of the bowl touch the water. Heat gently, stirring occasionally, until the chocolate is melted and smooth. Remove the bowl from the heat and let cool slightly.

Pierce a piece of fruit with a toothpick or skewer and dip it into the melted chocolate. Transfer to a sheet of waxed paper and let set for about 1 hour. Eat within 3–4 hours of coating.

scotch pancakes

index

conversion charts

Weights and measures have been rounded up or
down slightly to make measuring easier.

A US stick of butter weighs 4 oz. which is
approximately 115 g or 8 tablespoons.

Volume equivalents

American	Metric	Imperial
1 teaspoon	5 ml	
1 tablespoon	15 ml	
¼ cup	60 ml	2 fl.oz.
⅓ cup	75 ml	2½ fl.oz.
½ cup	125 ml	4 fl.oz.
⅔ cup	150 ml	5 fl.oz. (¼ pint)
¾ cup	175 ml	6 fl.oz.
1 cup	250 ml	8 fl.oz.

Weight equivalents

Imperial	Metric
1 oz.	25 g
2 oz.	50 g
3 oz.	75 g
4 oz.	125 g
5 oz.	150 g
6 oz.	175 g
7 oz.	200 g
8 oz. (½ lb.)	250 g
9 oz.	275 g
10 oz.	300 g
11 oz.	325 g
12 oz.	375 g
13 oz.	400 g
14 oz.	425 g
15 oz.	475 g
16 oz. (1 lb.)	500 g
2 lbs.	1 kg

Measurements

Inches	cm
¼ inch	5 mm
½ inch	1 cm
¾ inch	1.5 cm
1 inch	2.5 cm
2 inches	5 cm
3 inches	7 cm
4 inches	10 cm
5 inches	12 cm
6 inches	15 cm
7 inches	18 cm
8 inches	20 cm
9 inches	23 cm
10 inches	25 cm
11 inches	28 cm
12 inches	30 cm

Oven temperatures

250°F	120°C	Gas ½
275°F	140°C	Gas 1
300°F	150°C	Gas 2
325°F	160°C	Gas 3
350°F	180°C	Gas 4
375°F	190°C	Gas 5
400°F	200°C	Gas 6
425°F	220°C	Gas 7
450°F	230°C	Gas 8
475°F	240°C	Gas 9

recipe credits

Nadia Arumugam
Stir-fried vegetables with
five-spice tofu

Fiona Beckett
Extra-crispy mac and cheese
Mac 'n' greens

Vatcharin Bhumichitr
Egg noodles stir-fried with
vegetables and curry paste

Celia Brooks Brown
Chile greens with garlic crisps
Grilled asparagus and leaf
salad with sesame-soy
dressing
Minty grilled zucchini
Pad Thai noodles
Thai cole slaw
Tomato and bread salad
Warm chickpea salad with
spiced mushrooms

Tamsin Burnett-Hall
Bean and vegetable soup
Mustardy mushroom stroganoff
Pan-fried Caribbean bananas

Maxine Clark
Asparagus with Parmesan and
chopped eggs
Belgian leek tart
Classic Italian salad
Eggplant, tomato, and
Parmesan gratin
Grated cucumber, sour cream,
and paprika salad
Mushroom risotto
Spinach risotto with arugula
and roasted tomatoes
Tomato, mozzarella, and basil
salad

Linda Collister
Easy speedy pizza
Juicy fruit crisp
Strawberry tartlets
Tomato and red lentil soup

Ross Dobson
Almond and lemon cake
Asian-style tofu omelet
Asparagus, corn, and goat
cheese frittata
Baked cheesecake
Baked spinach mornay
Braised fennel with polenta
Broccoli and potato frittata
Cauliflower and caperberries on
halloumi
Cauliflower and Swiss chard
salad with chickpeas
Coconut creamed rice with
poached plums
Fresh tomato, pea, and paneer
curry
Garden salad with garlic toasts
Mozzarella and basil toasties
Nectarine and pistachio crumble
Orange vegetable and scallion
pilau
Pan plum crumble
Pasta with purple sprouting
broccoli, chile, and pine nuts
Pumpkin and Gorgonzola risotto
Pumpkin and feta packages
Raspberry and almond tart
Rhubarb and custard pots
Roasted early fall vegetables
with chickpeas
Smashed roast potatoes
Spaghetti with butternut squash,
sage, and Pecorino
Spaghetti with peas and mint
Spiced eggplant couscous
Spinach and cheese curry
Stir-fried tofu with crisp greens
and mushrooms
Tabbouleh with chickpeas and
spring salad
Upside-down tomato tart
Whole-wheat spaghetti with
zucchini and herbs

Clare Ferguson
Mixed vegetable tian
Penne with mozzarella, herbs,
and tomatoes
Spaghetti with tomatoes and
eggplant

Ursula Ferrigno
Broccoli and lemon risotto
Country-style risotto
Farmers' risotto
Fennel and lemon risotto
Risotto with eggplant, pine nuts,
and tomatoes
Risotto with lemon and mint
Tomato risotto

Liz Franklin
Big pasta shells stuffed with
herbs and ricotta
Creamy pea soup
Farfalle with zucchini, raisins,
and pine nuts
Penne with tomatoes and basil
Spaghetti with herbs and garlic

Manisha Gambhir Harkins
Eggplant and tomato stacks
Raw tomato and herb sauce on
grilled polenta
Warm goat cheese salad

Tonia George
Huevos rancheros
Couscous with roast squash,
halloumi, dates, and
pistachios
Omelet with chives and cheese

Brian Glover
Squash and sage frittata

Nicola Graimes
Cottage cheese pancakes with
sweet chili mushrooms
Lebanese halloumi salad
Lemon and spinach Puy lentils
with hard-boiled eggs
Soufflé cheese omelet
Strawberry sundaes
Summer fruit bars
Tofu and vegetable wraps
Zucchini, potato, and onion
tortilla

Kate Habershon
Triple chocolate pancakes

Rachael Anne Hill
Baked mushrooms
Chile pasta bake
Chocolate and hazelnut
brownies
Chocolate-dipped fruit
Creamy spinach
Double chocolate fruity squares
Feta-stuffed bell peppers
Ginger, rhubarb, and cream
cups
Homemade baked beans
Mozzarella-topped herby
vegetable loaf
Rice and bean burgers
Sesame sugar snap peas
Spicy lentil dip
Vegetable burritos
Warm potato salad

Caroline Marson
Lemon and herb feta salad
Roast tomato, goat cheese, and
arugula tartlets
Roasted butternut squash risotto
Roasted vegetable soup

Jane Noraika
Beefsteak tomatoes with garlic
and herb butter
Feta salad with sugar snap peas
Portobello mushrooms with
lemon and olive oil
Thrown-together olives,
tomatoes, and feta
Whole cauliflower with olives

Elsa Petersen-Schepelern
Baba ganoush
Chile and mint raita
Cucumber and ginger raita
French onion soup
Stir-fried mushrooms
Tomato, onion, and chile raita

Louise Pickford
Avocado salsa
Baked goat cheese on toast
Berries with honeyed yogurt
Chunky eggplant burgers
Coconut caramel sauce
Curried sweet potato burgers
Farfalle with roasted squash,
feta, and sage sauce
Melon with ginger syrup
Quick Mexican mole
Quick vegetable curry
Scrambled eggs with
mushrooms
Spiced falafel burgers
Stir-fried tofu with chili coconut
sauce

Tomato and olive tart with
Parmesan
White bean soup with olive
gremolata

Rena Salaman
Baked eggplant with garlic and
tomatoes
Zucchini fritters

Jennie Shapter
Grilled bell pepper frittata
Feta, tomato, and herb omelet
Indian omelet
Mushroom and bell pepper
tortilla
Roasted vegetable tortilla
Sweet potato and Brie tortilla

Fiona Smith
Apple and bulgur wheat salad
Crushed peas
Olive oil and garlic bread
Portuguese potatoes
Ratatouille
Tomato, avocado, and lime
salad with crisp tortillas

Sonia Stevenson
Roast butternut squash
Sweet potatoes skewers

Sunil Vijayakar
Cauliflower masala

Fran Warde
Avocado and chickpea salad
Baked fennel with shallots and
spicy dressing
Pappardelle with parsley
Poached mushrooms with egg
noodles
Warm Puy lentil salad

Laura Washburn
Apple cole slaw
Baked apples and pears
Greek omelet

Lindy Wildsmith
Black bean and avocado salad
Fusilli with tomatoey sauce
Lemon roast potato wedges
Linguine with ricotta, cinnamon,
and walnuts
Pasta with basic cream, butter,
and Parmesan sauce
Pasta with quick tomato sauce
Rigatoni with roasted vegetables
Scotch pancakes
Red kidney bean curry

photography credits

Key: a=above, b=below, r=right, l=left, c=center.

Richard Jung
Pages 2, 8, 11ar, 31, 38, 39a, 39c,
40, 54, 57, 62, 63a, 68, 82, 85,
86, 97, 106, 109, 114, 125, 129,
130, 167, 168, 175b, 179, 183,
187, 198, 204, 210, 211a, 215,
216, 224l, 226

Peter Cassidy
Pages 11al, 12-13bc, 13b, 16,
17b, 21, 47, 75, 87a, 91, 93r,
105a, 111r, 111, 117, 126, 134,
174, 184, 203, 207, 221

Martin Brigdale
Pages 3c, 12-13a, 35, 71, 138, 142,
157, 158, 175c, 176, 208, 235

Tara Fisher
Pages 1, 11bl, 15, 87b, 94, 105b,
153, 162, 165, 171, 195, 197

Nicki Dowey
Pages 11br, 18, 72, 76, 81, 98, 149,
154, 175a, 180

Diana Miller
Pages 3l, 13a, 32, 39b, 43, 44, 48,
51, 104, 122

William Reavell
Pages 3r, 5, 53, 87c, 88, 101, 121,
200, 222, 231

Jason Lowe
Pages 133, 137, 141, 145, 146,
188, 191

Lisa Linder
Pages 14, 63c, 63b, 64, 67, 79

William Lingwood
Pages 17a, 22, 261, 28, 232

Kate Whitaker
Pages 118, 211c, 211b, 219, 224r

Vanessa Davies
Pages 93l, 172, 212, 229l

Philip Webb
Pages 17c, 25, 37, 58

Jean Cazals
Pages 61, 102, 192

David Munns
Pages 12bl, 105c, 161

Jonathan Gregson
Pages 6, 151

Jeremy Hopley
Page 111l

Debi Treloar
Page 26r

Ian Wallace
Page 229l